PLATFORM EUROPE

SLOW TRAVEL EUROPE

PLATFORM EUROPE

UNFORGETTABLE TRAIN JOURNEYS
ACROSS THE CONTINENT

BART GIEPMANS & WILLIAM SIMPSON

ⓜ

FOREWORD

Europe by Train

We fell in love with travelling by train more than twenty years ago, almost without realising it. There were no grand plans or lofty ideals at the start, just a simple curiosity and a sense of adventure. One journey led to another, and before long that curiosity had carried us to places we never expected to find ourselves, like visiting vineyards on the slopes of Mount Etna, watching the midnight sun over Lapland, and waking in the Scottish Highlands at dawn.

Over the years, we realised that train travel changes the way you see Europe. From a motorway, the continent rushes past in fragments, and from a plane, it vanishes altogether. But from a train window, you see how it all fits together. Forests thicken, coastlines appear, cities emerge and fall away again. One country becomes another, and you hardly notice it happening.

Somewhere along the way, trains stopped being just a way of getting from A to B. They became the reason to travel to begin with. We started noticing more – landscapes, details, people. We struck up conversations we'd never have had otherwise. Some of our fondest memories come from these chance encounters, like a night train from Odesa to Lviv, where we spent hours talking with an elderly woman, sharing stories through gestures and smiles, despite not speaking a single word of the same language.

And then there are the stations. Europe has more than forty thousand of them. Some are vast and magnificent, others no more than a platform and a bench. But each one marks the beginning of a new journey, and nowhere in the world makes those beginnings as simple, or as inviting, as Europe.

With 250,000 km (155,000 mi) of track, you can travel from the Arctic to the Mediterranean, from the Atlantic to the edge of Asia, without ever leaving the ground. Get an Interrail or Eurail Pass, and 33 countries are yours to explore.

The routes in this book are ones we've travelled ourselves, often more than once. Some are well known, others rarely talked about. But we hope each of them inspire you to slow down, to watch the world pass by, and to remember that getting there can be just as fun as arriving.

Bart Giepmans and William Simpson

CONTENTS

01	Beyond the Arctic Circle – Stockholm to Narvik	13
02	Following the Rhine Upstream – Cologne to Oberalp Pass	29
03	The Road to Liberation – London to Berlin	45
04	Scotland's Highlands and Islands – London to Scotland	59
05	Via the Vineyards to the Côte d'Azur – Paris to Nice	73
06	Along Spain's Golden Coast – Montpellier to Valencia	89
07	The Riviera Line – Nice to Pisa	105
08	Wild, Wild Wales – London to Snowdonia	119
09	From the Alps to Mount Etna – Zurich to Catania	129
10	Heading East into Slovakia – Vienna to Košice	143
11	Steam Trains and Witches – Hannover to Harz Mountains	157
12	Over the Alps to the Adriatic – Frankfurt to Split	167
13	Above the Clouds at Jungfraujoch – Bern to Jungfraujoch	179
14	Poland, from the Baltic to the Tatras – Berlin to Zakopane	187
15	The Land of Lakes and Vineyards – Munich to Trento	197
16	The Pyrenees' Forgotten Station – Paris to Zaragoza	209
17	From the Seine to the Sahara – Paris to Marrakech	219

Epic Long-Distance Journeys	238
Mountain Adventures	240
Island Railways	246
Super Slow	251
Night Trains	259
Interrail & Eurail Passes	262
Index	270

01 SWEDEN – NORWAY

STOCKHOLM – NARVIK

Beyond the Arctic Circle

The reindeer appear without warning, trotting across the tracks ahead of us. Our driver brakes, the train slows to a crawl, then stops. Through the window we watch them pause mid-crossing, glance back with mild curiosity, then wander into the forest. The driver checks the line is clear and we roll forward again. Welcome to Sweden's Inlandsbanan, the Inland Line, where wildlife has right of way and nobody's in a hurry.

We've been travelling for days now, following a chain of trains deeper into Swedish Lapland: first an intercity to Mora, then the Inlandsbanan through the vast interior, and eventually the Iron Ore Line towards Norway. Our destination is Narvik, a small port on Norway's Arctic coast, more than 1,600 km (1,000 mi) north of where we began in Stockholm. By the time we get there, we'll have crossed some of the emptiest country in Europe, where in summer the sun barely sets and the forests go on forever.

A LINE THROUGH THE WILDERNESS

The Inlandsbanan runs for almost 1,300 km (800 mi) from Kristinehamn in central Sweden to Gällivare in the north, cutting straight through the interior and deliberately avoiding the coast. The idea emerged in the late 1800s, though it took three decades to complete. The reasoning was both strategic and economic: an inland railway would be harder to attack than a coastal line, and it would connect the sparsely populated but resource-rich north with the industrial south.

Constructing it was an extraordinary feat. The route winds through dense forests, peat bogs and river valleys, forcing engineers to build some 250 bridges and lay mile after mile of reinforced track. When the line finally opened in 1937, it should have been a triumph for Sweden. Instead, it was Germany that benefitted most.

Despite Sweden's official neutrality during the Second World War, the government allowed Nazi Germany to move troops and equipment north via the Inlandsbanan. By the early 1940s, some two million German soldiers had travelled this route, up to 12,000 each week, bound for occupied Norway.

By the 1950s the railway was in slow decline. Car ownership was rising across Sweden and a new motorway ran almost parallel to the tracks. Passenger numbers fell, and in 1992, the national railway declared the line financially unviable and announced its closure. After 55 years, it seemed destined to fade into history.

SAVING THE LINE

But the following year, fifteen municipalities along the route joined forces to form Inlandsbanan AB and took over operations. Today a handful of services run each summer from mid-June to late August. With just sixty seats per train, it feels more like a travelling living room than public transport.

Each train on this route has a train host, and ours quickly becomes part guide, part storyteller. She points out wildlife, shares local history, and explains the hazards of reindeer on the tracks. With more than 250,000 wild reindeer in northern Sweden, encounters are frequent. Trains often stop suddenly, wait for the herd to drift away, then creep forward again. Up here, nature sets the pace.

STATIONS AND STOPS

There were once around 200 stations on the Inlandsbanan. Most have closed and many buildings were sold. Today passengers can board at 29 official stations, plus a handful of request stops where the train pauses if you signal the driver. There's even a brief halt at the Arctic Circle, marked by a signpost, so everyone can step out for a photo and a breath of cold air.

While some people use the line simply to get from one place to another, most, like us, treat the journey as an experience in itself. They break it into stages, spending a night here, two nights there, exploring small towns and the vast wilderness along the way. Thanks to allemansrätten, Sweden's right of public access, you can also camp freely almost anywhere in the country.

MORA, OUR FIRST STOP

We plan seven stops between Stockholm and Narvik, and the first is Mora, on the shores of Lake Siljan. Formed by a meteorite impact millions of years ago, it's now one of Sweden's most beautiful lakes, ringed by forest and red-painted cottages.

Mora itself is known for two things, the first being Njupeskär, Sweden's highest waterfall, which falls 93 m (305 ft) through a narrow gorge in Fulufjället National Park. The second is the Dala horse, the brightly painted wooden toy that has become a symbol of Swedish handicrafts. In the nearby village of Nusnäs, artisans carve and paint around 120,000 each year.

The train departs Mora at 1:25pm sharp, and with only one daily service heading north, this is

one departure you don't want to miss. As we pull away and head deeper into the interior, the landscape grows wilder. The traditional red houses, coloured with faluröd paint made from mine waste, thin out. Soon there's only forest, mile after mile of pine and birch stretching to the horizon.

Our train host today keeps us entertained with stories and songs, and introduces us to fika, the Swedish ritual of slowing down over coffee and cake. Over the speakers she plays "Koppången," a haunting melody inspired by the landscape we're passing through.

Every so often we spot old water pumps standing alone among the trees. They're wartime relics, we're told, left from when German troop trains refilled their tanks here rather than in nearby villages, where soldiers might be tempted to desert. Our host talks about the secret movements of troops and weapons along this line, even mentioning *Schwere Bruno*, a massive railway gun that once rumbled through these forests. It's hard to imagine now, in a place so quiet and peaceful, yet the history still feels close to the surface.

HALFWAY NORTH

When we arrive in Östersund, it's raining, and although we're only halfway up the country, it already feels like the far north. Set on the shores of Lake Storsjön, which is said to be home to a monster not unlike Loch Ness, the town is known for its food, and as a UNESCO City of Gastronomy it lives up to its reputation, with cafés and restaurants across the centre serving both traditional dishes and modern Nordic cooking.

We spend the afternoon at Norra Station, a café, roastery and gallery, where the coffee is excellent and the atmosphere relaxed. Later we try Sav Glöd, a local birch wine made from sap tapped by hand and fermented into a crisp, earthy drink unlike anything we've tried before.

The only train north leaves at 7:40am, so we stay an extra night, giving ourselves time to walk the lakeshore and gear up for the journey into Lapland.

ENTERING LAPLAND

The next morning we continue to Storuman, the first stop in Swedish Lapland. It's a five-and-a-half-hour ride and the landscape grows wilder by the minute. We pass the former low-security prison at Ulriksfors, where inmates could come and go with relative freedom. "It's known as Sweden's first hotel," our train host jokes.

At Vilhelmina Norra, we stop for nearly an hour and head to Bergmans, a restaurant beside the tracks, for lunch. The speciality is Arctic char, simply cooked and very fresh. One of the pleasures of the Inlandsbanan is these generous stops in small places: time to eat properly, stretch your legs and speak to locals.

By the time we reach Storuman we're deep in the wild north. A century ago it was a small farming village, only growing into a regional centre when the Inlandsbanan arrived, which brought hydroelectric development and the timber trade. Today it's a quiet base for anyone seeking some peace.

A short walk from the wooden station, which dates to 1916, is Storumans Camping, where you can sleep in a traditional Sami kata (a kind of wooden tent) or in a log cabin overlooking the lake. We choose the cabin, and that evening climb Stenseleberget hill for views west to Norway's mountains on the horizon.

CROSSING THE ARCTIC CIRCLE

From Storuman the line continues to Jokkmokk, a six-and-a-half-hour journey through pine forests and marshland, over countless rivers flowing east to the Baltic Sea. This is some of the emptiest country in Europe and for hours we see only trees, water and sky.

After a while, we pass Sweden's smallest station at Buddnakk, little more than a wooden hut, then cross the Arctic Circle somewhere south of Jokkmokk. The marker is simple–just some white stones and a signpost. "They're not entirely accurate, though," our host tells us. "The Arctic Circle actually shifts a few metres each year. But it's close enough."

Soon after, the train stops again. A herd of reindeer is standing on the rails. The driver sounds the horn. Nothing. He waits, tries again, eases forward. At last the animals scatter into the forest. "We see everything up here," the driver tells us later. "Elk, lynx, sometimes even bears. Reindeer are tricky, though. They belong to Sami herders but behave like wild animals." If a train hits one, the railway pays compensation to the herder. It's a reminder that this is Sami land, where reindeer herding has shaped life for thousands of years.

SILENCE AND SOLITUDE

It's after eight in the evening when we pull into Jokkmokk, but the sun still hangs high. In summer this far north, darkness never quite comes. The sun dips for an hour or two around midnight, then climbs again. It's disorienting at first, the endless daylight, but you adjust.

When the train disappears north, silence falls over the platform. Jokkmokk Municipality is roughly the size of Wales yet has only about 5,000 residents. The town itself is just a handful of streets around a central square.

Jokkmokk has long been a meeting place for the Sami. The winter market each February has run since 1605 and remains one of the great cultural events of the north. In summer the town is a hub for outdoor activities: husky trips, fat-bike rides and wild camping, with Northern Lights tours in autumn.

We stay at the Peace & Quiet Hotel, a cluster of floating cabins on a forest lake a few miles from town. The owner, Björn, once trained Special Forces soldiers to survive in the wilderness for weeks at a time. Now he offers his guests a gentler version of solitude. That night we sit on the deck watching the light fade, though never disappear, listening to the water lap against the pontoons.

THE IRON ORE LINE

From Jokkmokk it's a short run to Gällivare, where you can also spend the night at the Grand Hotel

Lapland beside the station. This is the start of the Malmbanan, the Iron Ore Line, one of Europe's most important freight railways.

The line was built for a single purpose: to move iron ore from the vast mines around Kiruna to the coast. Iron had been known about here since the 17th and 18th centuries, particularly by the Sami, but extracting and transporting it at scale was impossible.

For centuries, only small quantities of ore travelled south by reindeer and boat, but everything changed when the railway opened in 1902. Ore could finally move in large volumes, cheaply and efficiently. The mines expanded, towns grew and the region was transformed.

Today, the railway runs from the coastal city of Luleå to Narvik in Norway, passing through Kiruna, Sweden's northernmost city. Kiruna exists because of iron, but its vast underground mine has brought both wealth and upheaval. As the ground has slowly sunk, the city has had to move, shifting around 4 km (2.5 mi) east, a relocation still in progress. In summer 2025, even the 672-tonne wooden church was carefully lifted and rolled to its new home.

Immense ore trains, some 800 m (2,625 ft) long, still thunder along the line to the ports, but passenger services share the tracks too, opening this once-remote region to travellers in a way that would have been unimaginable a century ago.

THE GATEWAY TO LAPLAND

Beyond Kiruna the line follows the shore of Lake Torneträsk, a long, narrow lake flanked by mountains. The water is blue-grey and in summer patches of snow still cling to the higher slopes. This is one of Scandinavia's most beautiful railway stretches.

Many hikers get off at Abisko, the southern gateway to the Kungsleden, the King's Trail, a 440-kilometre (273-mile) route through the mountains. The Abisko valley is spectacular: wildflower meadows, fast rivers and peaks rising steeply on all sides. In summer the sun shines at midnight for weeks. In winter the same latitude brings the Northern Lights.

We ride the chairlift to the Aurora Sky Station at 900 m (2,953 ft), a research and viewing site on the mountainside. From there a trail climbs to the summit of Mount Nuolja at 1,164 m (3,819 ft) for sweeping views over Lake Torneträsk and the Lapporten valley.

In the early twentieth century, when the railway first opened, people travelled all the way from Stockholm for this very same experience. But back then there was no cable car, and the journey took more than two days. For many visitors, it was the adventure of a lifetime, something to be remembered and retold. People used to set off up the mountain in their Sunday best – men in suits, women in long dresses – climbing slowly towards the same views we're enjoying now.

DESCENT TO NARVIK

The final stretch takes less than two hours, running from Abisko across the Norwegian border to Narvik. At Riksgränsen, Sweden's last station, the old locomotive depot has been reborn as Niehku Mountain Villa, a base for hikers, bikers, and skiers, its name meaning "dream" in the Sami language.

From Riksgränsen the track begins a dramatic descent to the coast. This stretch, the Ofoten Line, is Norway's northernmost railway and one of its most impressive, the rails clinging to cliffs high above the Rombaksfjord. When we finally roll into Narvik, more than 1,600 km (1,000 mi) from where we started, it feels like the edge of the world.

But Narvik is far from empty. Despite its size, this Arctic port of around 15,000 people has played a pivotal role in history. Its deep, ice-free harbour made it crucial to the iron ore trade, and during the Second World War the town saw fierce fighting. The Battles of Narvik in 1940 were among the most significant naval engagements in the early stages of the war, and the Narvik War Museum in the town centre tells the story well.

Beyond its wartime legacy, Narvik is also a gateway to the mountains. A cable car rises straight from the harbour to the heights above town, offering sweeping views of Ofotfjord and the peaks that surround it. We spend our final evening by the waterfront, watching the light shift over the fjord and thinking about our long journey through this remote corner of Europe.

From Narvik, a night train can take you back to Stockholm in a single 18-hour journey, or you can continue south into Norway by bus to Bodø, where the main Norwegian railway network begins. Either way, an adventure awaits.

JOURNEY DETAILS

Begins at Stockholm Central, Sweden
Ends in Riksgränsen or Narvik in Norway

Where you'll go
Stockholm can easily be reached by direct trains from Berlin, Hamburg, Oslo or Copenhagen.

Stockholm – Mora, 4 hours
Mora – Östersund, 5 hours
Östersund – Storuman, 7 hours
Storuman – Jokkmokk, 6 hours
Jokkmokk – Gällivare, 1.5 hours
Gällivare – Abisko, 3 hours
Abisko – Riksgränsen, 1 hour
Riksgränsen – Narvik, 1 hour

From Narvik, a night train runs back to Stockholm in one 18-hour journey, or you can continue south into Norway by bus to Bodø, then take the Nordlandsbanan to Trondheim and Oslo.

Time needed
Two weeks minimum, though three is better. The distances are huge, and there are plenty of places to stop for hiking or outdoor activities. Some sections between stations can be hiked as well.

Best time to travel
The Inlandsbanan's slow trains only run in summer (10 weeks from June until August). Abisko, which you can also reach by direct night train from Stockholm, is popular for Northern Lights viewing. Wild camping is allowed in Sweden, but summer is peak mosquito season, especially in Lapland.

Tickets & reservations
We used an Interrail/Eurail Global Pass (15 travel days in one month), which covers trains from Hamburg or Copenhagen to Stockholm, plus all trains in Sweden and Norway. Reservations are required from Copenhagen onward (Hamburg-Copenhagen only in summer). On the Inlandsbanan, there's only one northbound train per day at each stop, and reservations are compulsory.

02 GERMANY - SWITZERLAND

COLOGNE - OBERALP PASS

Following the Rhine Upstream

Stand on the banks of the Rhine anywhere between Rotterdam and Basel and you'll see a river at work. Barges push upstream against the current, passenger boats churn past, the water wide and busy. It powers industry, irrigates farmland, and shapes national borders. Hard to believe this vast waterway begins as a trickle in the Alps, small enough to step across without getting your feet wet.

This journey through the Rhine Valley has been a classic European route since the nineteenth century, when steamboats and railways first opened the region to travellers. Castles, cliffs, and vine-covered slopes came to define the romance of the river, celebrated by poets and painters and eagerly sought out by early tourists. For decades, it was simply the way to travel south through Germany.

Today, though, most people take the high-speed line. Since 2002, fast trains have raced from Cologne to Frankfurt in just one hour, bypassing the river entirely. It's efficient, no question, but the slower route along the water is by far the more beautiful. And if you want to understand why the Rhine inspired such devotion for so long, you must see it from the old line.

COLOGNE, THE RHINE AT ITS WIDEST

We begin in Cologne, where the river is at its most impressive, nearly half a kilometre wide and fast-moving through the heart of the city. Just before the train pulls into the central station, it crosses the Hohenzollern Bridge, Germany's busiest railway crossing. Through the window, Cologne Cathedral rises above the water, its darkened stone and soaring spires dominating the skyline.
If time allows – and it should – Cologne deserves at least a few hours. We leave our bags in the station's lockers and walk straight to the cathedral. This is Germany's most visited monument and the third tallest church in the world, a Gothic masterpiece that took more than six centuries to complete. The sandstone has darkened from centuries of soot and pollution, giving it a brooding feel. Inside, the scale is overwhelming. Stand in the

nave, look up, and you see why people have made pilgrimages here for generations.

THROUGH THE WINE VALLEYS

Trains run south along the Rhine several times an hour, and we take our time, hopping off whenever something catches our eye. In Bonn, Beethoven's birthplace is just a five-minute walk from the station, now a museum celebrating his life and music. At Remagen, the remnants of the Ludendorff Bridge jut into the river, a reminder of March 1945 when American forces captured it intact, hastening the end of the war. A small museum nearby tells the story in detail.

At Andernach, we take a brief detour to see the world's highest cold-water geyser, which shoots 60 m (197 ft) into the air. It's more novelty than spectacle, but still worth the stop.

All trains on this stretch eventually reach Koblenz, where the Moselle flows into the Rhine at a pointed headland called Deutsches Eck. A massive bronze statue of Emperor Wilhelm I on horseback stands at the tip. We walk out to where the two rivers meet, then take the cable car up to Ehrenbreitstein Fortress, high above the confluence, for views over the entire valley.

From Koblenz, we detour again along the Moselle towards Trier. The first section to Cochem is one of Germany's loveliest stretches of railway. The track curves with the river, passing steep vineyards, medieval villages and castles perched on rocky ledges. This also happens to be Germany's oldest wine region. The Romans planted the first vines here two thousand years ago, and today more than five thousand winemakers produce some seventy million litres of wine a year, much of it excel-

lent Riesling. We stop in the village of Winningen for a glass before returning to the Rhine.

CASTLES, CLIFFS AND THE LORELEI

South of Koblenz, the river enters its most dramatic section. This is the Upper Middle Rhine Valley, a UNESCO World Heritage Site where the river cuts through a narrow gorge between steep, forested hills. The train runs so close to the water we can see the current pushing against the bows of passing barges.

Just beyond St Goar we pass the Lorelei, a 132 m (433 ft) slate cliff rising above a particularly narrow and treacherous stretch of the Rhine. For centuries sailors feared this point: the current accelerates, the channel narrows and hidden rocks lurk under the surface. From that danger came myth. Heinrich Heine's poem about a siren luring sailors to their death is the best-known version, but the legend is much older.

The trains stop frequently along this route. We get off at Bacharach, a small town of half-timbered houses and cobbled lanes that looks unchanged for centuries. Bingen and Oberwesel are equally charming, each a good base for walks through the surrounding vineyards.

Wine enthusiasts should also look out for Bopparder Hamm, a great bend in the river lined with south-facing terraces that produce some of the valley's best Rieslings. Sheltered by the Hunsrück hills, this little microclimate has nurtured vines for millennia. We buy a bottle from a small estate near the tracks and tuck it into our bag.

MAINZ AND THE GUTENBERG MUSEUM

Mainz, an ancient city with a lively modern centre, sits at the confluence of the Rhine and the Main. It's known as Germany's wine capital, and we spend an evening in one or two of its wine bars, sampling bottles from the very regions we've been travelling through. But Mainz's real claim to fame is Johannes Gutenberg. Just off Liebfrauenplatz, the Gutenberg Museum celebrates the

man who invented movable type and changed the course of history. Inside are early presses, trays of metal type and beautifully preserved examples of early printed books, including pages from the Gutenberg Bible. It's a small museum but a fascinating one, and it makes you appreciate just how radical Gutenberg's idea truly was.

From Mainz, fast trains run directly to Basel and into Switzerland, but we're not ready to leave Germany just yet. Instead of following the Rhine south, we make a small detour and head towards the Black Forest. It means leaving the river behind for a while, but the reward is worth it. Heidelberg is less than an hour away, and it's far too beautiful to skip.

A DETOUR TO HEIDELBERG

Heidelberg survived the Second World War almost unscathed, a rare stroke of luck that preserved its old town. Today it's one of Germany's most picturesque cities: red roofs, narrow streets, and Renaissance façades climbing the banks of the Neckar.

We take the funicular up to the castle ruins, vast and atmospheric, with sweeping views across the valley. Then we follow the Philosophenweg, or Philosophers' Way, a gentle path along the hillside where Goethe and countless other poets and thinkers once walked. The panorama over the old town is well worth the hike.

THE BLACK FOREST RAILWAY

From Heidelberg it's a quick hop back to Karlsruhe, where we board the Schwarzwaldbahn, the Black Forest Railway. This double-decker regional train follows one of Germany's most scenic lines along the northern edge of the Black Forest. When we eventually set off, the landscape opens almost immediately. To the west the Rhine Valley spreads out, to the east the dark ridges of the Black Forest rise in the distance. On clear days you can see all the way to the Vosges Mountains in France.

The three-hour journey is slow and soothing, passing vineyards, half-timbered villages and quiet countryside. After Baden-Baden the train winds through Gengenbach, one of those impossibly pretty German towns with a medieval centre and a centuries-old town hall. Beyond Triberg, the line descends towards the headwaters of the Danube, still just a stream at this point. We get off at Singen and transfer to a train for Schaffhausen, a short ride away, and there the Rhine shows us one of its greatest spectacles.

EUROPE'S LARGEST WATERFALL

The Rhine Falls is one of the few waterfalls with not one, but two railway stations. We get off at Neuhausen Rheinfall, a tiny platform, and follow the signs to the viewing platforms.

The falls aren't particularly high, only 23 m (75 ft), but the volume is astonishing. Up to 600,000 litres per second thunder over the rocks, making this Europe's most powerful waterfall. You can take a boat right up to the base, but even from the platforms the sheer force is impressive. The noise, the spray, the relentless surge of water. It's exhilarating. Even the onward ride from Schaffhausen to Zurich is scenic. Make sure you sit on the left for the best views.

ALONG LAKE WALEN

The journey from Schaffhausen to Chur takes just two hours, with a quick change in Zurich. The trains are fast and modern, but it's the scenery that makes the journey special. First, we skim along the southern shore of Lake Zurich, then cut inland before emerging beside Lake Walen.

For the next half hour, the train hugs a narrow strip of land between sheer cliffs and turquoise water, with forests rising steeply on the opposite shore. Even by Swiss standards, this feels pristine.

SWITZERLAND'S GRAND CANYON

Chur is where the Alps begin in earnest. We board a red Rhaetian Railway train, part of the network that serves southeastern Switzerland, and begin climbing into the high country. The line follows two tributaries of the Rhine – the Hinterrhein and Vorderrhein – heading deeper into the mountains with every mile.

Between Reichenau and Ilanz the train runs through the Rhine Gorge, sometimes called the Swiss Grand Canyon. A prehistoric landslide carved this narrow valley, leaving pale white cliffs that rise up nearly 400 m (1,315 ft). The river runs fast below, and we spot canoeists riding the rapids. It's a UNESCO World Heritage Site and one of Switzerland's most spectacular rail journeys, which is already saying something.

At Disentis/Mustér we change to the Matterhorn Gotthard Railway for the final climb to the Oberalp Pass. At 2,044 m (6,706 ft), this is one of the highest railway crossings in the Alps. The pass marks the border between the cantons of Grisons and Uri, and in late summer, when the snow has melted and wildflowers scatter the meadows, the views are extraordinary.

WHERE THE RHINE BEGINS

From the Oberalp Pass, a marked trail leads to Lake Toma in about two hours. It's not a difficult walk, though the altitude makes the ascent slow. The path climbs steadily through alpine meadows and boulder-strewn slopes, following the Vorderrhein upstream.

Lake Toma sits in a high mountain bowl at 2,345 m (7,694 ft), a deep blue pool ringed by snowy peaks and scree. This is officially the source of the Rhine. Meltwater from surrounding glaciers trickles into the lake, then flows out as the Vorderrhein, which later joins the Hinterrhein to form the river proper.

Standing here in near silence, it's hard to believe this water will travel through six countries, past dozens of cities, and eventually reach the North Sea. The Rhine supplies drinking water to thirty million people, supports vast industries and agriculture, and carries more freight than almost any other river in Europe. But climate change threat-

ens its future: glaciers are shrinking, snowmelt is decreasing, and water temperatures are rising, altering the river's flow in ways that could affect us all.

Still, on this bright afternoon beside Lake Toma, those concerns feel distant. We fill our bottles with icy water, take one last look at the lake and the mountains, and step across the infant Rhine in a single stride.

JOURNEY DETAILS

Begins at Cologne Hauptbahnhof, Germany
Ends at Oberalp Pass, Switzerland

Where you'll go
This route mostly follows the Rhine upstream, with a detour through the Black Forest. Alternatively, you can travel via Basel, which is highly recommended, or choose the longer, slower route along Lake Constance, where regional trains hug the shoreline and stop at highlights such as Stein am Rhein and Konstanz.

We started at Cologne Hauptbahnhof, a major hub with direct connections to Amsterdam, Brussels, Paris and Berlin.

Cologne – Koblenz, 1.5 hours
Koblenz – Heidelberg, change at Mannheim, 2 hours
Heidelberg – Schaffhausen/Rheinfall, change at Karlsruhe and Singen (Rheinfall station is 4 minutes from Schaffhausen), 4 hours
Schaffhausen – Chur, change at Zurich, 2 hours
Chur – Oberalp Pass, change at Disentis/Mustér, 2 hours

From Oberalp Pass, you can head back to Chur and reach Zurich in an hour. Or follow the Glacier Express route using local trains to Brig and Zermatt.

Time needed
Five days minimum, though you could easily fill two weeks. It's about a 2-hour walk from Oberalp Pass station to Lake Toma, the source of the Rhine.

Tickets & reservations
A flexible Interrail/Eurail Pass (7 days within one month) gives you plenty of freedom for spontaneous stops and train hopping. The pass covers the entire route, and seat reservations aren't required anywhere. You could technically reach the source from Cologne in a day, but with so much to see along the way, a week makes more sense.

03 UNITED KINGDOM — FRANCE — GERMANY — CZECHIA — POLAND - GERMANY

LONDON - BERLIN

The Road to Liberation

This journey traces the path of Europe's liberation during World War II, from the English ports where the D-Day landings were planned, by ferry to the beaches of Normandy, and onwards by train to Berlin, where the conflict came to its conclusion. Spanning more than 3,000 km (1,865 mi), it passes through some of the most consequential sites of the 20th century.

For many of the more than 150,000 Allied troops who landed on five French beaches on 6th June 1944, the journey began years earlier, training in the forests of southern England, on land the army had requisitioned and closed off from the outside world. Evidence of those hidden preparations survives to this day. So too does the Atlantic Wall, the chain of Nazi fortifications that stretches along the coast of continental Europe, its concrete remnants still scattered across the beaches on the other side of the Channel.

Our journey to trace this history begins at London Waterloo. During the war, the grand terminus served as a departure point for servicemen heading south to the staging grounds of Operation Overlord, the Battle of Normandy. We board a train along the same route those soldiers once travelled, arriving in Portsmouth ninety minutes later.

The Queens Hotel, a stately Edwardian landmark that once counted both Churchill and Eisenhower among its guests, serves as our base. From here we visit Southwick House, the Victorian manor where Eisenhower established his headquarters. Still an active military facility, access requires prior arrangement, but those who make it inside will find the wooden wall map used to plan D-Day hanging exactly as it did on the morning Eisenhower gave the order to go.

TRACES OF WAR

By bus, we pass through Creech Wood. During the war, this forest served as a marshalling area for British and Canadian troops awaiting deployment. The remains of their camp still lie hidden among the trees, the same site that, after the invasion succeeded, was converted to hold German prisoners of war.

Our final stop in Portsmouth is The D-Day Story, Britain's only museum dedicated solely to the Normandy campaign. Its centrepiece is the Landing Craft Tank 7074, one of the very boats that carried soldiers onto the beaches that June morning, and the last surviving vessel of its kind in the country.

The following morning, we board a Brittany Ferries crossing to Ouistreham, sailing almost the same route the Allied fleet took on D-Day. As the French coastline slowly emerges, the beaches come into view – quiet stretches of sand where thousands landed, and from which many never returned.

6TH JUNE 1944: D-DAY

We disembark and make our way to Caen, a city all but destroyed by Allied bombing. Today, the Mémorial de Caen stands on the site of a former German command post. Rather than focusing solely on weapons and tactics, the museum examines the human toll of the conflict. Two films play on a loop: the first, D-Day, honours the 90,000 soldiers and 20,000 civilians who died in Normandy; the second, Europe our history, reflects on how easily peace can be lost.

From Caen, tours run to the landing beaches. The drive takes us along narrow country roads, past countless plaques and monuments. The hedgerows lining the fields look ordinary enough now, but in 1944 they formed a dense maze that slowed the Allied advance to a crawl. Many paratroopers landed miles from their intended drop zones and pushed through this landscape in darkness, never knowing what waited behind the next hedge.

THE BEACHES

Standing on the sand, the chaos of D-Day feels impossible to fully grasp. The heaving sea, the crack of machine-gun fire, the desperate scramble for cover. Omaha Beach saw the heaviest fighting. Of the 35,000 Americans who came ashore here on 6th June, some 4,700 were killed, wounded, or went missing. It quickly became known as Bloody Omaha. A short distance along the coast, the cliffs at Pointe du Hoc remain pitted with bomb craters, the ground so scarred it looks almost lunar.

The cemeteries are just as affecting. At Colleville-sur-Mer, more than 9,000 American graves overlook the sand where so many fell. Across Normandy, American and Commonwealth cemeteries impress with grand monuments and heroic symbolism, while German cemeteries, such as La Cambe, are notable for their understated simplicity and quiet dignity.

A CITY ALMOST DESTROYED

From Caen, in just two hours we're in Paris, a city that in 1944 came dangerously close to destruction. As the Allies advanced, Hitler ordered the entire city to be levelled. Explosives were placed beneath the bridges over the Seine, in the Louvre, the Palais Royal, the university and even beneath the Eiffel Tower. The order was clear. If Paris couldn't remain German, it shouldn't remain at all.

The task fell to Dietrich von Choltitz, the newly appointed military governor. He faced an impossible choice: disobey Hitler, or destroy one of the world's great cities. In the end, he stalled, secretly negotiating with the Allies until it was too late to carry out the demolitions. On 25th August, he surrendered Paris largely intact.

A highlight of our visit is the Musée de la Libération de Paris in the 14th arrondissement. Dedicated to Resistance leaders Jean Moulin and Henri Rol-Tanguy, it brings the story of the city's liberation to life. Using augmented-reality headsets, we step into the underground command post where crucial decisions were made and experience the battle for liberation in a startlingly immersive way. You hear the gunfire, see the barricades, feel the tension of those final days before freedom.

PROPAGANDA AND JUSTICE

The train from Paris to Nuremberg, with a change in Frankfurt or Stuttgart, takes about six and a half hours, giving us time to read about what followed liberation.

Long before it hosted the post-war trials, Nuremberg was one of the symbolic centres of Nazi power. Hitler admired its medieval architecture, which he believed embodied an eternal German spirit, and he staged vast rallies here to project the image of a unified Reich.

On the city's southern edge are the former Nazi Party Rally Grounds, a vast site that remains deeply unsettling. The stone grandstand where Hitler addressed the crowds still stands, as does the half-finished congress hall, designed to hold

50,000 people. Even the parade avenue, the Große Straße, was aligned so that Nuremberg Castle would rise dramatically at its far end, though ironically, that straight road later helped guide British bombers during night raids.
The Nuremberg Trials ran from November 1945 to October 1946, seeking justice for crimes almost unimaginable in their scale and cruelty. Of the 24 defendants, twelve were sentenced to death, of whom ten were executed. Courtroom 600, with its wooden benches and gallery, is now a museum.

BRUTAL REPRISALS

The fastest route from Nuremberg to Kraków runs through Leipzig, but we take the longer way, via Prague. It's a city of spires and cobbled squares, yet beneath its beauty lies a dark chapter of wartime history.
In May 1942, Reinhard Heydrich was the Reich Protector of Bohemia and Moravia. A high-ranking SS officer and one of the architects of the Holocaust, he ruled with such brutality that he became known as the Butcher of Prague. On 27th May, two resistance fighters – Jan Kubiš and Jozef Gabčík, both trained by British Special Operations – ambushed Heydrich's open-top Mercedes in the district of Libeň. Kubiš threw a modified anti-tank grenade, mortally wounding Heydrich, who died eight days later.
The German retaliation was swift and brutal. More than 13,000 people were arrested, at least 5,000 were murdered. The villages of Lidice and Ležáky were razed to the ground, the men shot, the women deported to concentration camps, the children killed or given to German families for "Germanisation." The assassins hid in the crypt beneath the Church of Saints Cyril and Methodius in central Prague. On 18th June, betrayed by a collaborator, they were surrounded by 800 SS troops. After hours of fighting, with no hope of

 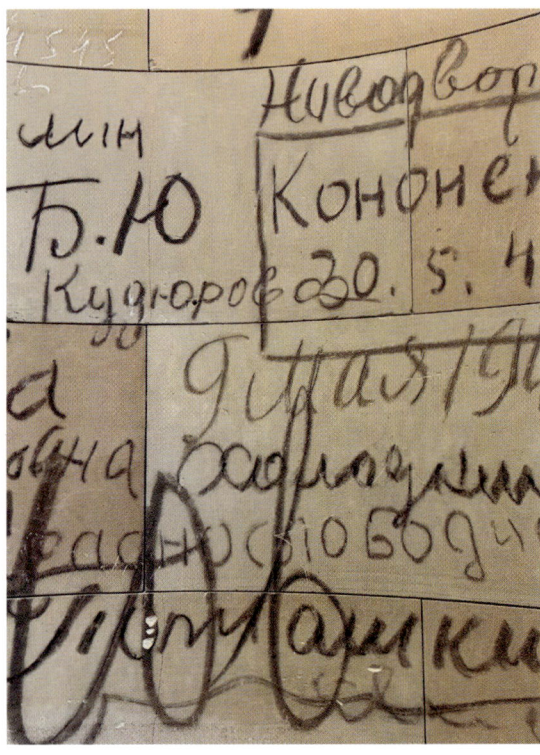

escape, they took their own lives. The bullet holes are still visible in the walls outside the church. The paving stones are engraved with the date of the battle, and inside the crypt, now a memorial, photographs of the fighters hang in silence.

SCHINDLER'S FACTORY

From Prague we continue to Kraków, the former royal capital of Poland. It's a beautiful city – Romanesque churches, Gothic towers, Renaissance courtyards – but it sits in the shadow of one of history's darkest places, Auschwitz. Oskar Schindler's name is widely known thanks to Spielberg's film, and his former enamelware factory in the district of Podgórze is now a powerful museum. A plaque outside bears the Talmudic verse made famous by the film: *"Whoever saves one life, saves the world entire."*

Our guide tells us about another hero, Tadeusz Pankiewicz, the only non-Jewish pharmacist allowed to remain in the Kraków Ghetto after it was sealed. He provided medicine, shelter and information to residents, often at immense personal risk, and his small pharmacy became a meeting point for the Resistance.

'THOSE WHO DO NOT REMEMBER THE PAST...'

The local train from Kraków to Oświęcim takes around ninety minutes, and we grow quieter with every passing moment. When we arrive, we walk to Auschwitz I in near silence. Nothing really prepares you for it. A guide tells us how the smell from the crematoria drifted over the town, how ash sometimes fell from the sky. People assumed it came from chimneys or factories. Then the truth emerged.

A sign lists the numbers: 1.1 million people murdered here, ninety per cent of them Jewish. Many were killed within hours of arrival. Inside the gas chamber, we look up at the opening where the Zyklon B pellets were dropped. The room is small,

the ceiling low. It's unbearable to imagine it how it once was used. Behind glass displays we see piles of belongings: shoes, suitcases, glasses, pots, pans. Even human hair. Everything was taken. Even here, the Nazis found ways to profit from murder.

A shuttle takes visitors to Auschwitz-Birkenau, the largest of all the camps, its perimeter ringed by miles of electrified fencing. Most of the wooden barracks have since been destroyed, leaving only the chimneys standing like gravestones across vast empty fields. A cold wind sweeps the site. In winter, flimsy uniforms and unheated barracks offered almost no protection. Those not murdered in the gas chambers often died of disease, starvation or exposure.
At the end of the railway line stands the memorial, inscribed with words that feel more urgent now than ever: "*Those who do not remember the past are condemned to repeat it.*"

THE BATTLE OF BERLIN

The next morning we board a Polish Intercity train for the seven-and-a-half-hour journey to Berlin After yesterday, it feels like an enormous luxury just to sit quietly and watch green countryside roll past the window. Before we know it, we're pulling into Berlin Hauptbahnhof, the end of our journey. Berlin fell to the Soviets in early May 1945 after one of the war's most ferocious battles, and the city is still marked by it.
From the station platforms, the Reichstag is visible, a short walk today but in April 1945 a deadly stretch of ground defended to the last. The Moltkebrücke bridge just north of the station was heavily fortified by SS troops and Volkssturm militia. After days of brutal street fighting, the Red Army raised its flag above the Reichstag on 2nd May, signalling the beginning of the end.

GERMANY SURRENDERS

In the eastern suburb of Karlshorst, we visit a modest villa surrounded by tanks and artillery. It was here, just after midnight on 9th May, that the German high command signed the act of unconditional surrender. Inside, the German Russian Museum presents an unflinching exhibition on Operation Barbarossa and the Eastern Front. In the surrender room, the flags of the four Allied powers hang exactly as they did that night. Afterwards, we visit Treptower Park, home to the largest Soviet war memorial in Germany, honouring more than 80,000 Soviet soldiers who died in the battle for Berlin. At the entrance stands a solemn statue of a grieving mother. At the far end, a colossal figure of a Soviet soldier carries a rescued German child while crushing a broken swastika underfoot.

A CITY THAT REMEMBERS

Our journey ends at the ruins of Anhalter Bahnhof. Once one of Europe's grandest stations with trains departing for Vienna, Rome and Athens, now only a fragment of its façade remains, a quiet memorial to everything that was lost. Nearby, an exhibition titled *Hitler: How Could It Happen?* explores how democracy collapsed and how ordinary people became complicit. It's a place of reflection, and it feels like the right place to finish.

JOURNEY DETAILS

Begins at London Waterloo, England
Ends at Berlin Hauptbahnhof, Germany

Where you'll go
You can reach London by direct Eurostar from Amsterdam, Brussels or Paris.

London Waterloo – Portsmouth, 1.5 hours
Portsmouth – Caen, ferry, 6 hours
Caen – Paris, 2 hours
Paris – Nuremberg, change in Stuttgart or Frankfurt, 7 hours
Nuremberg – Prague, change in Schwandorf, 4.5 hours
Prague – Kraków, 6 hours
Kraków – Berlin, 7 hours

Berlin is a major hub with direct connections to Amsterdam, Paris, Copenhagen, Stockholm, Prague, Budapest, Vienna, Warsaw and Zurich.

Time needed
At least 10 days to do justice to each location, though two weeks is better. These are all major destinations with plenty to offer beyond WWII history.

Tickets & reservations
An Interrail/Eurail Global Pass (7 or 10 travel days within one month, or 15 consecutive days) is ideal for this route. Seat reservations are compulsory on most trains, including the Eurostar to London.

LONDON – SCOTLAND

Scotland's Highlands and Islands

The far north of Scotland is one of Europe's last true wildernesses. Granite mountains rise above windswept moors, heather colouring the hillsides a deep purple. Peat bogs stretch to the horizon. Sea stacks stand in some of the roughest waters on Earth. Getting here is part of the adventure, too.

Our train from London to Inverness doesn't leave until late evening, so we walk down Euston Road to St Pancras, one of London's great Victorian Gothic buildings. Inside, Booking Office 1869 occupies the station's original ticket hall. It's a grand space, with vaulted ceilings, polished wood panelling, and a long turquoise bar complete with palm trees, and we enjoy an early dinner.

Afterwards, we duck next door to the The Martini Bar for a cocktail. It's moody, with green velvet banquettes and dim lighting, the kind of place Victorian travellers might have calmed their nerves before a long journey. If you're going to start an adventure, this is how to do it.

BOARDING THE CALEDONIAN SLEEPER

By half past eight, passengers are gathering for the two Scottish sleepers leaving that night. We show our tickets to a uniformed attendant and make our way down the platform.

A sleeper service has connected London and Scotland since 1873, and it remains as exciting and romantic a journey as it must have been then. The Caledonian Sleeper offers several options. Our Classic Rooms are small but well designed. Fabric-lined walls muffle the sound, reading lights adjust easily, and on the pillow sits an amenity kit with an eye mask and earplugs. Before turning in, we head to the Club Car. It's already filling up, passengers settling in with whisky or wine. The menu is proudly Scottish, haggis included, but we order a cheeseboard and a local beer. The train shudders and begins to move, and we start sliding through central London, past lit office windows and the dark mass of Regent's Park. Back in our

cabins, we watch the last streetlights fade, rooftops giving way to black countryside. By the time sleep comes, we've crossed half of England.

WAKING IN THE HIGHLANDS

When we wake, everything has changed. Hills emerge from low-hanging cloud, small lakes glint in the early light. I pull back the curtain and watch fields of yellow gorse and purple heather glow in the morning sun.

The train pushes north, deeper into the Highlands, past forests and salmon rivers running fast and dark. Every few minutes, a tiny station appears and vanishes again, and we fight the urge to jump off and explore.

An hour before Inverness, there's a knock at the door. A steward stands in the corridor with a tray: coffee, orange juice, a warm pastry. We eat breakfast watching Scotland roll past, the light growing brighter, the hills greener, until we slow into the capital of the Highlands.

INVERNESS

The morning is cool and clear when we step onto the platform, and with a few hours to spare before our next train, we walk along the River Ness, which flows from Loch Ness a few miles to the south. The water is glassy, reflecting the cathedral spires and the sandstone walls of Inverness Castle. One stop is essential: Leakey's Bookshop, Scotland's largest secondhand bookshop, housed in a converted church. Shelves climb to the ceiling, a wood-burning stove crackling in the corner. We browse for an hour and leave with something to read on the train.

THE FAR NORTH LINE

Back at the station, we board a ScotRail train for Thurso. The Far North Line is one of Britain's most remarkable railways, four hours through some of the most remote country in Europe. The carriage is quiet. A few locals, a couple of hikers with heavy backpacks. This isn't a tourist route, not yet at least.

The train pulls out of Inverness, and the suburbs fall away within minutes. Stations appear and disappear. The most unexpected stop is Dunrobin Castle, which was built as a private platform for the Duke of Sutherland and still today only operates during castle opening hours. The castle itself is extraordinary, a fantasy of turrets and towers right on the coast, white walls gleaming against the grey North Sea. Dating to the early 1300s, it's one of Britain's oldest continuously inhabited houses. We press the request button, hop off, and explore the castle and its grounds for a few hours.

THE FLOW COUNTRY

Beyond Dunrobin, the line turns inland and enters a landscape unlike any other. The Flow Country is a vast expanse of blanket bog, dark pools and mounds of green and yellow moss stretching to the horizon. It looks empty, but this peatland is a vital ecosystem, storing around 400 million tonnes of carbon, more than twice that held by all of Britain's forests. It was awarded UNESCO status in 2024.

The train moves slowly through this delicate terrain, the only sign of human presence being the track ahead and behind. We watch in silence, trying to absorb the strangeness of it all.

THURSO AND THE EDGE OF BRITAIN

Thurso is the northernmost town on the British mainland. "That small grey town by the sea," as the Scottish poet George Mackay Brown called it, and the description is fair. But the coastline is what draws people here. In the nineteenth century, this remote corner was an industrial powerhouse. Flagstones quarried in nearby villages paved streets in London, Edinburgh, Sydney, even Wall Street.

Later that day, we take a detour to Dunnet Bay, where the North Sea meets the Atlantic at the Pentland Firth, known for some of the strongest tides on Earth. The result is spectacular wave-bat-

tered sea stacks like those at Duncansby Head. The Duncansby Stacks rise 60 m (200 ft) from the churning water, jagged pillars of rock capped with grass, surrounded by wheeling seabirds. We stand at the cliff's edge, buffeted by wind, watching waves crash below. It feels like the edge of the world.

JOHN O'GROATS AND THE CASTLE OF MEY

John O'Groats is a small village near the northern tip of the mainland. Its name comes from Jan de Groot, a Dutchman who operated a ferry to Orkney in the 1400s. Today the village is little more than a car park and a gift shop, but the views across the Pentland Firth are worth the detour, Orkney low and grey on the horizon. Far more interesting is the Castle of Mey, a few miles along the coast. The Queen Mother bought it in 1952 for £100 and set about restoring it, filling the rooms with a mix of comfort and style. And although the Queen jokingly called it "Mummy's draughty castle," it feels welcoming rather than grand. Charles and Camilla still visit each summer.

CROSSING TO ORKNEY

At dawn the next morning, we're at the ferry pier in Scrabster, down the road from Thurso, waiting to cross the Pentland Firth. The crossing takes about an hour, and the water lives up to its reputation, the sea heaving even on a calm day. We stand on deck as the mainland shrinks behind us, salt spray on our faces, watching Orkney grow closer. The Old Man of Hoy comes into view, a 137-metre (450 ft) sea stack rising from the cliffs.
People have lived on Orkney for at least 5,000 years, and the evidence is everywhere. Our first stop is Skara Brae, a Neolithic village preserved beneath sand dunes until a storm stripped them away in 1850. What emerged was astonishing: stone houses with beds, shelves, dressers, even a primitive drainage system, all predating the pyra-

mids. We walk the raised pathways, looking down into the ruins where families lived and slept five millennia ago.

The Ring of Brodgar is equally atmospheric. Twenty-seven stones remain of the original sixty, standing in a circle between two lochs. We arrive in late afternoon, when the shadows are long, and walk slowly around the perimeter.

SCAPA FLOW

Orkney's history extends far beyond the Neolithic. During both World Wars, the islands served as a strategic naval base. Scapa Flow, the natural harbour at the centre of the archipelago, sheltered the British fleet, and it's here, in 1919, that one of the strangest events in maritime history took place. At the end of the First World War, the German High Seas Fleet was interned at Scapa Flow pending peace negotiations. Fearing the ships would be seized by the Allies, Admiral Ludwig von Reuter gave a secret order to scuttle the fleet. On a June morning, German sailors opened the seacocks and within hours, over 50 warships had slipped beneath the surface.

Many were later salvaged, but several wrecks remain on the seabed, drawing divers from around the world.

LOCH NESS, FORT WILLIAM AND BEN NEVIS

Back in Inverness after our journey to Orkney, we set out on the West Highland Line south toward Glasgow. To reach it, we take the bus to Fort William, pausing at Loch Ness along the way where the 13th century Urquhart Castle is worth an

hour or so. Fort William sits at the head of Loch Linnhe, surrounded by some of the most dramatic scenery in Scotland. The town itself is unpretentious, but it serves as the gateway to Ben Nevis, the highest peak in the British Isles, which at 1,345 m (4,413 ft) draws thousands of hikers each year.

THE GLENFINNAN VIADUCT AND STATION

Next morning, we're on the platform for the train to Mallaig. This stretch of the West Highland Line is famous for one thing above all: the Glenfinnan Viaduct. Twenty-one arches, 30 m (100 ft) high, curving across a Highland glen. You know it even if you've never been to Scotland, because it's the route of the Hogwarts Express in the Harry Potter films. In summer, steam trains run this section for the full cinematic experience, but regular ScotRail services cross the viaduct year-round, and our Interrail passes work fine. As the train slows onto the viaduct, everyone crowds the windows, cameras at the ready. Below, the River Finnan winds through the valley. Scotland, we decide, is best seen from a train.

The station at Glenfinnan was nearly demolished in the 1990s, but locals saved it and today it houses a small museum about the history of the line. Better still, you can spend the night in a converted 1958 railway carriage parked beside the platform, with wood-panelled walls, comfortable bunks, and a window looking towards the mountains.

INTO THE WILDERNESS

From Fort William, we board a southbound train towards Crianlarich. There's no phone signal here, just the landscape. And what a landscape it is. The train climbs steadily, the hills growing starker, until we reach Rannoch Moor. Rannoch is a vast, empty peat bog, and building the railway across it was no small feat of engineering. The track had to be floated on layers of turf and brushwood to stop it sinking. Even now, the line seems impossibly fragile, a thin thread crossing a landscape that looks like it wants to swallow it.

CORROUR

The train soon slows, then comes to a stop in the middle of nowhere. We're at Corrour, the highest and most remote station in Britain. The platform is a strip of concrete in an ocean of moorland, 408 m (1,339 ft) above sea level and 16 km (10 mi) from the nearest road. Corrour is famous for the scene in Trainspotting where the characters tumble off the train into this beautiful emptiness, bewildered by the silence. Today, a couple of hikers step onto the platform and walk off into the moor without looking back. The whistle blows and we're moving again, leaving Corrour to its solitude.

JOURNEY DETAILS

Begins at London Euston
Ends in Inverness, Glasgow or Fort William

Where you'll go
You can reach London by direct Eurostar from Amsterdam, Brussels or Paris.
London Euston – Inverness, night train, 12 hours
Inverness – Thurso, 4 hours
Inverness – Fort William, bus, 2 hours
Fort William – Mallaig, direct with stopover at Glenfinnan, 1.5 hours
Fort William – Glasgow Queen Street, 4 hours

Time needed
At least a week, especially if you want to visit the Orkney Islands. Key stops include Inverness, Thurso, Fort William and Glenfinnan. You can take the overnight Caledonian Sleeper from London to Inverness, then continue on the Far North Line to Thurso, Britain's northernmost station. Alternatively, get off at Glasgow and take the West Highland Line north to Fort William and Mallaig, one of the world's great scenic rail journeys.

Tickets & reservations
We used an Interrail/Eurail Pass (7 days within one month), which covers travel to and within the UK. For the Caledonian Sleeper, an additional reservation is required. Alternatively, consider a BritRail or BritRail Scotland Pass. In northern Scotland, buses are a convenient option: stagecoachbus.co.uk.

05 FRANCE

PARIS - NICE

Via the Vineyards to the Côte d'Azur

For this journey, we hop on a southbound regional train, following the vineyards of Burgundy and the Rhône's wide curve. From the window, green hills give way to red cliffs and eventually flashes of turquoise water. By the time we reach Nice after four days, it's clear the slower route was worth it.

GATEWAY TO THE SOUTH

We usually take the fast TGV from Paris to Marseille. Three hours and you're done. You board, read a bit, drift off, and before you know it you're by the Mediterranean. Even walking into Paris Gare de Lyon feels like stepping partway to the Mediterranean. The great hall is lined with murals of sunlit southern towns – Menton, Toulon, Montpellier – reminders that trains from here have carried travellers south for more than 170 years, ever since Napoleon III opened the Paris–Lyon–Méditerranée line in 1849.

The familiar voice of the long-time SNCF announcer drifts through the station, reeling off an impenetrable string of numbers. We speak French reasonably well, yet still are completely baffled. *"Le train TER numéro dix-sept-mille-neuf-cent-quatre-vingt-douze…"* Why not just say where the train's going? It remains a mystery.

THE TRANS EUROP EXPRESS

In the 1950s and 60s, travellers from Gare de Lyon boarded the Mistral, the crown jewel of the Trans Europ Express network. It offered a fast, elegant link between Paris, Marseille and Nice, with comforts that seem almost extravagant today: two restaurant cars, a bar, a bookshop, even a hairdresser. For a time, it was the fastest train in Europe.

But the arrival of the TGV in 1981 brought that golden era to an end. Speed won out over style, and the Mistral disappeared. What remains is its route – and that's what we've come to follow, slowly, by regional trains.

To do that, we leave Gare de Lyon and walk fifteen minutes south to the far less glamorous Paris-Bercy. There's no grandeur here, just concrete, platforms and commuters. But it's the start of a beautiful journey all the same.

THROUGH FORGOTTEN STATIONS

A little after half past seven, we board the direct regional train to Beaune. It runs non-stop to Sens, covering the first 120 km (75 mi) at a brisk pace. In just an hour, Paris has slipped away, replaced by the forests of Fontainebleau and then the broad valleys of the Seine and Yonne. Beyond Sens, the train slows, stopping at quiet stations with romantic names: Laroche-Migennes, Nuits-sous-Ravières, Les Laumes-Alésia. In the age of steam, Migennes was a vital refuelling depot and a crossroads for trains heading south to Italy or east into the Alps. Today, only the faded Hôtel Le Terminus hints at that former glory, the platforms overgrown with weeds.

THE VINEYARDS OF BURGUNDY

The countryside grows greener as we approach Dijon, but we stay onboard, eager to reach the vineyards. Soon the Côte de Nuits appears in the morning light – those world-famous slopes of Chambertin, Vosne-Romanée, Corton – neatly terraced hillsides that produce bottles worth hundreds, sometimes thousands. A little further south, where the Côte de Nuits becomes the Côte d'Or, we reach Beaune, the wine capital of Burgundy and our first real stop.

WINE AND HISTORY IN BEAUNE

From the station, it's a short walk into Beaune's cobbled centre, a mix of honey-coloured stone, quiet lanes and wine shops. We visit Domaine Chanson Père et Fils for a tasting in their old cellars. Their finest wines are priced accordingly, but even the more modest bottles are excellent. Later, we wander through the vineyards themselves. Much of the work here is still done by hand, barely ten per cent mechanised. You feel that patience and precision in every glass. Before dinner, we slip into the fifteenth-century Hôtel-Dieu, once a hospital for the poor and now one of France's most beautiful museums. We arrive just before closing and find ourselves alone, walking through vast medieval halls in near silence.

FOLLOWING THE SAÔNE AND RHÔNE

The next morning, we catch a train to Lyon. Beyond Chalon-sur-Saône, the line follows the river, sometimes hidden behind poplars, then suddenly revealed in broad, shimmering bends. Then, just before Lyon Part-Dieu, the train crosses the water and offers a perfect view of the Basilica of Notre-Dame de Fourvière on its hilltop, standing watch over the city. Lyon takes food seriously. You can spend an afternoon learning how to bake pastries at the Institut Paul Bocuse, but we find ourselves at a traditional *bouchon lyonnais* instead, a local restaurant with chequered tablecloths, quenelles in cream sauce, and perhaps the richest praline tart we've ever tasted. After two hours, we roll back to the station and board the TER to Marseille.

The Rhône guides us now. Past Saint-Rambert-d'Albon, the valley narrows and the vineyards return. The train hugs the riverbank, passing abandoned stations with cracked plaster and grass growing between the tracks. Near Avignon, the view opens suddenly: volcanic hills in the distance, fields of sunflowers in the foreground. Avignon is tempting, but Arles is calling.

IN VAN GOGH'S FOOTSTEPS

Stepping off the train in Arles, the scent of wild lavender drifts from the tracks. Van Gogh arrived here in 1888 intending only to change trains but stayed for more than a year, captivated by the light. It's easy to see why. Everything feels warm-edged and luminous. We visit some of the places he painted: the Café Terrace on Place du Forum (immortalised in his *Café Terrace at Night*), the Roman amphitheatre, the stone viaduct. There's also a Saturday market to wander, small galleries to browse, coffee to drink under plane trees. By afternoon, the station pulls us back. Marseille awaits.

ARRIVAL IN MARSEILLE

Eventually we climb into Marseille-Saint-Charles, set high above the city. From the forecourt, we see the Mediterranean glinting between the rooftops, the Basilica of Notre-Dame de la Garde towering above it all. The grand staircase drops more than a hundred marble steps to the streets below where, at the bottom, Café l'Ecomotive offers the perfect pause before exploring.

Marseille isn't conventionally pretty, but it's endlessly compelling. Le Panier, the old quarter, is full of street art and small studios. The Museum of European and Mediterranean Civilisations (MuCEM), a lace-patterned concrete marvel, is connected to the old Fort Saint-Jean by a footbridge over the water. Then there's Cours Julien, where the city's creative crowd hangs out, bars and cafés spilling onto the streets.

We also stop at the Mémorial de la Marseillaise, a small but interesting museum about France's national anthem. The song was originally known as the "War Song of the Army of the Rhine", but volunteer soldiers from Marseille sang it on their march to Paris in 1792, and the name changed. "Vivre libre ou mourir" – live free or die – rings in our ears as we leave the museum, and craving a change of pace, we take a bus to Vallon des Auffes, a tiny fishing harbour tucked between cliffs, where we eat bouillabaisse as boats creak in the late afternoon breeze.

THE CÔTE BLEUE

Before heading to Nice, we decide to take a detour along the Côte Bleue, a small stretch of coastline located west of Marseille. A local train runs from the city to Miramas, hugging the coastline for 30 km (19 mi). The line is squeezed between sea and limestone cliffs, passing through the Calanques National Park with views that make you want to hop off at every station. Eventually we do, walking a section of the Sentier des Douaniers, an old customs path once used to catch smugglers. It twists between cliffs and coves, the smell of wild thyme and rosemary hanging in the air.

TOWARDS NICE

The next day, we board a train east. The rolling stock is older – former first-class carriages with spacious compartments and faded blue upholstery – a quiet echo of the Mistral's elegance. After Bandol and Saint-Cyr-sur-Mer, the train runs right along the water, close enough that you feel you could touch it. From Toulon, the line swings inland again, then back to the coast. The best views begin near Saint-Raphaël, where the red volcanic cliffs of the Esterel glow in the late light. The train slows, giving you time to take in the Anthéor Viaduct, the harbours of Mandelieu-la-Napoule, and cove after cove of blue water. Plan ahead if you want to stop, as only a few trains call at these tiny stations each day.

A TOUCH OF GLAMOUR

Soon we pass Cannes and Juan-les-Pins, though their glamour doesn't particularly entice us. The line curves around the Baie des Anges and then, at last, we arrive in Nice, the Queen of the Riviera and our final destination. After a day spent watching the Mediterranean through train windows, we're keen to go for a swim, so we drop our bags at the hotel and head straight for the Promenade des Anglais, the beach, and a glass of cold rosé. The journey from Paris has taken five days. It could have been three hours, but we're glad it wasn't.

From Nice, if you're still craving views after hours of spectacular scenery, the Train des Merveilles climbs to Tende, a beautiful village high in the Alps. Alternatively, the narrow-gauge Train des Pignes runs north towards Digne-les-Bains through wild, empty country. But that's for another day.

JOURNEY DETAILS

Begins in Paris Gare de Bercy
Ends in Nice Ville

Where you'll go
Paris – Beaune, 3.5 hours
Beaune – Arles, change in Lyon, 5 hours
Arles – Marseille, 1 hour
Marseille – Nice, 2.5 hours

Time needed
You could do Paris to Marseille in 10 hours (changing twice in Lyon and Avignon) without the TGV, but there are too many temptations along the way: Dijon, Beaune, Lyon, Orange and Arles. Give yourself at least a week.

Tickets & reservations
We used an Interrail/Eurail One Country Pass for France and avoided high-speed trains entirely, taking only regional TER services. With an Interrail Pass, it's effortless: no reservations needed and complete freedom to hop on and off. A TER train even runs from Avignon all the way to Portbou in Spain (see page 88).

06 FRANCE – SPAIN

MONTPELLIER – VALENCIA

Along Spain's Golden Coast

We leave Montpellier early, boarding the slow regional train south toward Portbou, just over the Spanish border. The morning light is soft and golden, and the Mediterranean feels close as soon as we pull out of the station. Empty beaches slide past, a lone cyclist follows the shore, and just before Agde, the first flamingos appear, standing motionless in the shallow waters.

After passing the locks at Mandirac, the train runs along a narrow strip of land with water on both sides. In the distance, the Pyrenees rise into view, the snow-covered peak of the Canigou massif following us almost all the way to the border. The French coast looks its best in this early light: salt lakes, small towns, and orchards reaching almost to the platform. We stay close to the shoreline until just beyond Port-la-Nouvelle, and two hours later we roll into Perpignan.

The high-speed line continues south from here, reaching Barcelona in less than an hour and a half. Most passengers change trains, but we stay on board the regional service. The old coastal route takes almost four times longer, but beyond Argelès the tracks squeeze between the mountains and the sea. It skirts the Mediterranean in unhurried fashion, past Collioure, Banyuls-sur-Mer, and Cerbère winding past rocky coves and quiet stations where the platforms are covered in yellow wildflowers. It's exactly the kind of rustic charm we travel for.

A STATION BUILT FOR BORDERS

The pace slows as the line threads its way into the eastern Pyrenees, before arriving at Portbou, a small border town defined by an outsized station, wedged between two mountain ridges. Portbou was once a major railway hub, with direct trains to Paris, Barcelona and Madrid, but its importance faded with the arrival of the high-speed rail link between Perpignan and Figueres, which opened in the early 2010s, allowing passengers to cross from

France to Spain far faster and without the ritual at the border.

The station, tucked into a deep fold in the mountains, still feels like a place where once borders mattered. It's huge for such a small town. In its heyday it housed everything from police, customs offices, ticket halls and cafés, all beneath a beautiful domed roof that dates to 1929. The old clocks from that era still tick away, and customs officers still patrol for smugglers, judging by the thorough checks we got on both legs of our journey.

A PLACE OF REFUGE

On the French side of the station, under a long canopy, you'll find two international tracks and a pair of platforms where French trains end their journey. The Spanish side has eight Iberian-gauge tracks, four of them under the main roof. Spain supposedly chose a different track gauge to make a French invasion more difficult.

Because of its location on the French border, Portbou – like nearby Cerbère – became a place of refuge many times during the twentieth century. After Franco's victory in the Spanish Civil War in 1939, thousands of Republicans fled over the nearby Coll dels Belitres into France. Nearly 100,000 crossed the border at Portbou alone, part of a vast wave of refugees fleeing persecution. One of the most extraordinary walks in the region begins at Banyuls-sur-Mer and crosses the Pyrenees to Portbou. It follows the same escape route used by those fleeing Nazi-occupied Europe, among them the German-Jewish philosopher Walter Benjamin as depicted in Netflix's Transatlantic). It's a difficult climb today, winding past vineyards with the Mediterranean stretching out endlessly beside you, but in 1940 it was a lifeline. A memorial to Benjamin, who took his own life here fearing arrest, stands just above the water and is deeply moving.

DALÍ, GIRONA AND THE RUN SOUTH

The next morning, after an espresso by the bay, we catch the regional R11 towards Barcelona Sants. The first major stop is Figueres, birthplace of Salvador Dalí and home to his wonderfully eccentric Dalí Theatre-Museum – a must-visit if you enjoy bold, colourful art. From there the

train rolls on to Girona, where the bright houses along the Onyar River appear just as we pull in. In ten minutes you can stroll to Plaça de la Independència, a square lined with cafés and terraces, and have a drink before wandering into the old town.

SITGES AND THE MEDITERRANEAN COAST

At Barcelona Sants we switch to the coastal train towards Sant Vicenç de Calders. As we leave the city, a sudden storm sweeps in, heavy rain lashing the windows. The train shudders to a halt, and within minutes the platforms have flooded. People start chatting, swapping stories. An elderly woman in our carriage laughs, saying she's never seen anything like it.

Soon the sky clears and the coastline comes back into view, so close that waves sometimes splash up onto the tracks. Sitges, about half an hour south of Barcelona, is the perfect place to pause. Known for its nightlife and easygoing charm, the town somehow feels both lively and unhurried. Whitewashed fishermen's cottages cluster around the old church on the headland, and the car-free promenade stretches for kilometres along the sea. We stop for lunch at Cinnamon, a vegan spot in the old town, and realise instantly that Sitges deserves at least one night, if not more.

TARRAGONA

South of Sitges, the train again runs so close to the beach you feel as though you could step straight onto the sand. At Tarragona we change trains and wander briefly through the old town. Below the Balcón del Mediterráneo a long golden beach stretches out, and the surrounding lanes are packed with small cafés and restaurants. Once we leave the city, the landscape becomes agricultural again. Orange groves appear first, then fields of dragonfruit and avocados.

South of the Ebro delta, the train reaches Vinaroz and Benicarlo. We both have childhood memories of long summers here, and something about this part of Spain always feels familiar. As evening approaches, we stop for the night in Benicarló, and the next morning continue south, passing Peñíscola Castle on its rocky headland, as dramatic as ever.

A STATION FULL OF ORANGES

Just outside Sagunto, a vast hilltop fortress appears, its long stone walls stretching across the hillside. This is where Hannibal and his army – elephants included – once stopped before marching on Rome. The climb is steep but rewarding, with wide views over the town, the orange groves and the blue sea glinting in the distance.

As we approach Valencia, the futuristic curves of the Ciudad de las Artes y las Ciencias come into view. Designed by Santiago Calatrava, this sweeping complex of museums, gardens and gleaming white buildings is proof that the city is close. The train slows as it reaches Estació del Nord, giving us time to take in the station. The modernist building is a celebration of Valencian agriculture, with colourful mosaics, intricate ironwork and references to oranges everywhere you look. Tickets are still sold from small windows set into a vast oak-panelled wall. Step outside and you're already in Ruzafa, one of Valencia's most vibrant neighbourhoods, a tangle of colourful streets, cafés, boutiques and small squares.

A GREEN MEDITERRANEAN CITY

Valencia has everything that makes a city easy to love: a warm Mediterranean climate, a compact historic centre, wide sandy beaches and, unlike Barcelona, room to breathe. It's also one of Europe's greenest cities. The Turia Gardens – a large urban park created in a dried-up riverbed – run through the city with shaded paths perfect for walking and cycling. Renting bikes is simple, and with more than 150 km (93 mi) of dedicated cycle lanes, the city feels safe to ride through.

One of our favourite routes leads out to Lake Albufera, Spain's largest freshwater lake, surrounded by rice paddies and traditional thatched houses called *barracas*. The ride is flat, ideal for a warm afternoon, and there are plenty of places to stop for a swim along the way.

But Valencia's commitment to sustainability goes beyond just its parks and cycle paths. Many of its beaches hold the European Blue Flag for environmental quality, and the city is home to Spain's first Green Michelin Star, awarded to the Ricard Camarena Restaurant for its focus on local ingredients and minimal waste.

After our ride, we find a spot on the terrace at Café de las Horas and order a jug of Agua de Valencia, a mix of gin, vodka, cava and, of course, freshly squeezed orange juice. We sit for a while in the sun, then wander back through the streets, ready to see what else the city has to offer.

JOURNEY DETAILS

Begins at Montpellier Saint-Roch
Ends at Valencia Estació del Nord

Where you'll go
Montpellier is easily reached by TGV from Paris.

Montpellier – Portbou, 3 hours
Portbou – Barcelona (stops at Figueres and Girona), 2.5 hours
Barcelona – Sitges, 30 min
Sitges – Tarragona, 30 min
Tarragona – Benicarló, 2.5 hours
Benicarló – Valencia, 2 hours

Time needed
At least a week. You could reach Barcelona quickly from Montpellier or Perpignan by high-speed train, but the slower coastal route offers so much that it would be a shame not to make frequent stops and spend time along the Mediterranean.

Tickets & reservations
We used a 7-day Interrail/Eurail Global Pass (valid within one month). No reservations are needed for the slow local trains. Renfe suburban trains (Rodalies) are also valid for Interrail / Eurail passholders. However, the Rail Planner app doesn't provide timetable data, so these routes have to be added manually.

07 FRANCE – ITALY

NICE – PISA

The Riviera Line

The appeal here is simple: the sea, all day long. More than 350 km (220 mi) of track run almost entirely within sight of the Mediterranean, sometimes so close you can smell the salt spray through the open windows.

Travellers have been drawn to the Mediterranean since the earliest days of train travel, to its warmth, its food, its mix of cultures and coastlines. By the 1860s the railways had reached Nice and Genoa, and within a few decades the region had become one of Europe's premier destinations. From 1897 until the First World War, you could board the Riviera Express in Amsterdam or Berlin and travel straight to Nice or Monte Carlo without changing trains, arriving in time for dinner and a night at the casino. The wealthy flocked south to escape cold northern winters, building extravagant villas along the shore and transforming once-quiet fishing villages into fashionable resorts.

That era of luxury expresses has long passed, though, overtaken by high-speed trains that race through the landscape without pausing. But the slower local services remain, and they leave far more room to explore: medieval hill towns, baroque churches, grand villas, working harbours, markets piled with focaccia and fresh herbs, and endless glimpses of blue water between the rocks. And with no reservations required, you can travel entirely on impulse—exactly the way this coastline deserves to be seen.

THE CÔTE D'AZUR

At Nice-Ville station we board a TER to Ventimiglia, the last stop before Italy. This double-decker train hugs the coast the entire way, stopping at ten small stations. We find seats upstairs on the right-hand side for the best sea views. The scenery is spectacular from the outset, with rocky headlands and small beaches tucked between cliffs.

Within minutes we're gliding into Villefranche-sur-Mer, a village so lovely we make a snap decision and get off. From the platform, the whole harbour opens below us, its ochre façades clustered around the water, fishing boats and yachts at anchor, a long curve of beach sweeping to the west. It's one of those Mediterranean scenes that looks almost implausibly perfect.

VILLEFRANCHE-SUR-MER

We wander into the old town through narrow lanes, the most intriguing of which is the Rue Obscure, a covered passage built in 1260 that still feels genuinely medieval. Originally designed so soldiers could move around unseen, it later served as a wine cellar, a livestock shelter and, during the Second World War, an air-raid shelter. Its atmosphere is so well preserved that it has been used as a film set several times, and it even appeared in U2's music video for *Electrical Storm*.

Down by the waterfront, we find a table at La Voile Bleue, a restaurant tucked beneath the railway line, order coffee, swim in the clear water just metres away, and then sit in the sun watching the village come to life. Re-energised, we walk along

the coast path to Cap Ferrat, one of the wealthiest postcodes on the planet. The peninsula is dotted with palatial Belle Époque villas hidden behind high walls. Two of the grandest, Villa Ephrussi de Rothschild and Villa Kérylos, are open to the public. The former was built in the early 1900s by Béatrice de Rothschild and houses her extraordinary art collection, while the villa itself is surrounded by nine themed gardens overlooking the sea. The latter is a meticulous recreation of an ancient Greek villa, complete with mosaics, frescoes and period furniture.

BEAULIEU, MONACO AND MENTON

We continue on foot to Beaulieu-sur-Mer, another small town with a fine beach and a lively morning market right beside the station, and from here we hop on the next train east. The line runs close to the sea, ducking in and out of tunnels as it rounds headlands.

Then, near Monaco, the train dives underground and stays there for the length of the principality. Monaco's geography presented a problem for the railway. The terrain is steep, the land valuable, and space almost non-existent. The solution, therefore, was to put the railway underground. The entire 1.7-kilometre stretch of track inside Monaco runs through a tunnel, with the station, Monaco-Monte-Carlo, buried deep beneath the rock. It's a strange experience, arriving in one of the world's most glamorous places and seeing nothing but concrete tunnel walls.

Back in daylight, we roll into Menton, the final French town before Italy. Known for its lemons, it hosts an annual citrus festival each February, complete with enormous sculptures made entirely from fruit. But what drew us here is the Promenade Le Corbusier, a cliffside path that leads to Cap Martin. It takes about ninety minutes end to end, past coves accessible only on foot. Plage du Buse is one of the prettiest, a quiet pebble beach wedged between rocks.

The path also passes two architectural landmarks. Villa E-1027, designed by Eileen Gray in the late 1920s, was one of the pioneering works of

modernist architecture. Le Corbusier admired it so much he built his own tiny cabin nearby, the Cabanon, a 15-square-metre (160 square-foot) wooden structure where he spent his final summers.

CROSSING INTO ITALY

At Ventimiglia we cross into Italy. The town is pleasant, especially on Fridays when the market spills through the streets and locals from Nice cross the border to stock up on olive oil and parmesan. But we're only here to change trains, switching from the French TER to an Italian Regionale bound for Genoa.

It's the slower of the two eastbound options, stopping at sixteen stations and taking just over two hours. But it stays close to the coast almost the entire time, offering some of the trip's finest views. We grab a quick espresso at the station bar before boarding. Italian regional trains rarely have on-board dining, but coffee from a counter is always excellent.

FADED GLAMOUR

Twenty minutes later we reach San Remo. Once the star of the Ligurian Riviera, it attracted European royalty escaping cold winters. Russian tsars, British aristocrats and wealthy industrialists all built villas here and traces of that elegance remain. Art nouveau buildings, a palm-lined seafront promenade, even a grand casino that once rivalled Monte Carlo's.

In contrast, San Remo's station is utilitarian and rather charmless, set back from the sea and hemmed in by modern development. The original station, right on the waterfront, closed decades ago when the railway was moved inland to allow for double track.

But that abandoned railway has found a new life as the Pista Ciclabile del Ponente Ligure, a 24-kilometre (15-mile) cycle path with the Mediterranean on one side and the Maritime Alps on the other. It passes through old railway tunnels and small seaside towns that have barely changed in decades, like Arma di Taggia, Riva Ligure and Santo Stefano al Mare. You can hire a bike in San Remo, ride as far as you like, then catch a train back from any station.

THE UNDERRATED COAST

Leaving San Remo, we watch a succession of beaches glide by, blue parasols lined up in neat rows on the sand. Some stations seem to be practically built on the beach itself, their platforms only metres from the water. At Borghetto Santo Spirito and Loano, you can practically step straight into the sea.

We break the journey in Albenga, a town that remains surprisingly overlooked despite being one of the most atmospheric on this stretch of coast. Its medieval centre is a tight grid of cobbled lanes, stone towers and Romanesque churches, and it was even once called the "city of a hundred towers," though by our count only a few survive.

One stop before Albenga is Alassio, a resort town and the starting point for a stretch of the ancient Roman Via Julia Augusta, the road that once linked Rome with southern France. The path climbs into the hills above the sea, offering superb views of the coastline and the island of Gallinara. Further along the line you'll also find Savona, a working port with an excellent waterfront promenade and, above it, the vast Fortezza del Priamar. It served as a prison for centuries, its most famous inmate being Giuseppe Mazzini, the revolutionary who helped unify Italy.

PALACES AND ALLEYWAYS

Approaching Genoa, the train passes through docks, shipyards and a seemingly endless number of suburban stations. We get off at Genova Piazza Principe, one of the city's two main stations. Opened in 1860, just as Italy was being unified, it was designed to impress, with marble columns, classical sculptures and decorative archways. Stepping inside feels a little like entering a palace. Genoa doesn't get the attention Florence or Venice do, which is a shame in our view. The historic centre is a tangle of narrow alleys, medieval towers and baroque churches all leading up to Via Garibaldi, a street of Renaissance palaces so grand it's a UNESCO World Heritage Site in its own right. Down by the water, the harbour has also been completely reinvented by Renzo Piano, Genoa's most famous architect, with museums, concert halls and public spaces now filling the old docklands. After a quick visit to the Casa di Cristoforo Colombo, the reconstructed home of the world-famous explorer, we head east along the coast to Boccadasse, a former fishing village, and sit on the rocks with gelato, watching the sun go down.

CINQUE TERRE, THE FAMOUS FIVE VILLAGES

South of Genoa, the train enters Cinque Terre, one of Italy's most dramatic stretches of coastline. Its name, "Five Lands", refers to the five clifftop villages along the shore: Monterosso, Vernazza, Corniglia, Manarola and Riomaggiore. A network of footpaths links the five villages, routes once used by farmers and fishermen moving between terraces and harbours. The most famous is the Sentiero Azzurro, the Blue Trail, a 12-kilometre (7.5-mile) path that climbs above the sea through vineyards and olive groves. Walking the full length takes five to six hours, but most people do it in sections, hiking between two villages and then catching the train to the next.

We hop off at Vernazza, perhaps the most photogenic of them all. A small harbour curves beneath tall, colourful houses, with a medieval watchtower guarding the rock above. In the late-afternoon light, as fishing boats putter back with their daily catch, it feels like one of the most perfect scenes on the Italian coast.

PISA AND THE LEANING TOWER

From La Spezia, the last major town before leaving the coast, it's about an hour to Pisa. The line cuts inland through flat farmland, a stark contrast to the cliffs and coves we've followed for days. As we get closer, anticipation starts to build. Some landmarks are so famous you wonder whether they can still surprise you.

From Pisa Centrale, it's a thirty-minute walk to the Piazza dei Miracoli, the Square of Miracles, where the tower stands beside the cathedral and baptistery. We cross the River Arno, wander medieval streets lined with cafés and gelaterias, and finally reach the square. It's crowded, of course – every tourist striking the same pose – but the tower itself is astonishing, its marble shining in the sunlight, leaning far more dramatically in person than I'd imagined.

We find a café on the edge of the square, order a lemon granita sorbet, and watch the slow swirl of visitors. After travelling the coast for days, sitting here with a cold drink feels like exactly the right way to finish.

JOURNEY DETAILS

Begins at Nice Ville, France
Ends at Pisa Centrale, Italy

Where you'll go
Nice Ville is easily reached by TGV from Paris.

Nice/Villefranche – San Remo, change in Ventimiglia, 1.5 hours
San Remo – Albenga, 45 min
Albenga – Genoa, 1.5 hours
Genoa – Pisa, change in La Spezia, 3 hours
Pisa Centrale has direct connections to Milano Centrale and Roma Termini.

Time needed
Nice to Pisa can be done in a single day with three changes (Ventimiglia, Genoa and La Spezia). It takes around six and a half hours. But this route is best enjoyed slowly. Two countries, four trains, and over 60 stations where you can hop off on a whim and find yourself on an empty beach or in a medieval village barely touched by tourism.

Tickets & reservations
French tickets from Nice to Ventimiglia can be bought via sncf-connect.com or at the station. Italian tickets from Ventimiglia onward can be bought via trenitalia.com or at any station. Regional trains are inexpensive and reservation-free. You can also use an Interrail/Eurail Pass. The Italia In Tour pass is valid for 3 or 5 consecutive days of unlimited travel on Trenitalia regional trains throughout Italy.

08 UNITED KINGDOM

LONDON - SNOWDONIA

Wild, Wild Wales

Northwest Wales can feel a world away from the rest of Britain. Mountains rise straight from the sea here, their slopes marked by centuries of slate quarrying. Medieval castles stand guard on clifftops, built near even older Celtic sites. In the villages, you're more likely to hear Welsh than English. Yet for all its remoteness, getting here is easier than you might expect. From London, a four-hour train ride brings you to Wales' western edge where the Cambrian Coast Line winds northwards, mountains on one side, the Irish Sea on the other, in one of the most naturally beautiful corners of the country.

CROSSING INTO WALES

We board an early train at London Euston on a warm July morning, the carriage almost empty. At Birmingham International, we change to a Transport for Wales service heading west, and as we pull away the announcements turn bilingual. "Diolch am deithio gyda Trafnidiaeth Cymru." Thank you for travelling with Transport for Wales. In north Wales where we're heading, Welsh isn't a heritage curiosity. It's the language of everyday life, spoken by more than two-thirds of the population.

The Cambrian Main Line was built in the mid-nineteenth century to connect the industrial Midlands with the coastal towns of west Wales. It cuts straight across the country, climbing through the Cambrian Mountains before descending to the sea. At Dovey Junction, the line splits, one branch continuing south to Aberystwyth, the other heading north along the coast to Pwllheli, forming the Cambrian Coast Line.

We unfold a map and trace our route, muttering station names under our breath: Llwyngwril, Dyffryn Ardudwy, Penrhyndeudraeth. Our Welsh

could use some work. As we cross the border, the landscape changes. We're passing through sparsely populated country now, sheep-farming territory where villages grow smaller and more scattered. The mountains ahead grow closer.

ABERYSTWYTH

Aberystwyth sits at the southern end of the Cambrian Coast Line, an old university town wedged between hills and sea. It has the slightly faded grandeur of a classic British resort, with a long promenade, a Victorian pier, fish-and-chip shops doing steady business.

We walk up to the ruined castle on the headland, then take the cliff railway – the longest electric cliff railway in Britain – to the top of Constitution Hill. The coastal path is wind-battered but the views stretch for miles. Below, families wander arm in arm along the front, coats zipped against the breeze.

ABERAERON

A short bus ride south brings us to Aberaeron, one of the prettiest towns on the Ceredigion coast. Unlike most Welsh villages, Aberaeron was a planned Georgian settlement built in 1807. The result is unexpectedly elegant, with terraced houses painted in soft pastels – pale blue, lilac, coral, butter yellow – arranged around a small harbour where fishing boats bob at anchor.

We walk along the quay, watching gulls ride the wind and dive for scraps. When rain sweeps in from the sea, we duck into a deli on the harbour front, where the owner greets us with samples of Welsh cheese and wine made from Welsh grapes. "This part of Wales isn't exactly the south of France," she says, pouring us a measure of seaweed-infused gin that turns out to be surprisingly good. "But we manage." We buy a bottle and step back into the drizzle.

ALONG THE CAMBRIAN COAST

The next morning, we board a northbound train at Aberystwyth. The Cambrian Coast Line runs roughly every two hours in each direction, just frequent enough to make spontaneous exploration possible. Our first stop is Aberdyfi, a village on the northern shore of the Dyfi estuary. To reach it, the train veers inland, skirting the Dyfi National Nature Reserve, a vast expanse of marsh and mudflat and one of the most important wetlands in Britain.

We pause briefly at Dovey Junction, surely one of the loneliest stations in the country – a single platform surrounded by reeds, the nearest road more than a mile away. In summer, birdwatchers come here to spot ospreys fishing the estuary.

Aberdyfi itself is small and charming, with a long curve of golden beach. It's also a village with an outsized place in Welsh history. For centuries, Welsh chieftains gathered here to settle disputes and forge alliances. In 1404, at a parliament held in these hills, Owain Glyndŵr was proclaimed Prince of Wales, the last native-born Welshman to hold the title. His rebellion against English rule would shake the country for fifteen years. He was never captured, never surrendered. He simply vanished into the mountains, becoming a legend.

A VILLAGE ON BORROWED TIME

Further north, the train passes through Fairbourne, a village caught in the crosshairs of climate change. With sea levels rising and storm surges growing more frequent, the cost of maintaining the village's defences has become prohibitively expensive. Officials even announced that in thirty to forty years, the village may need to be "decommissioned", its residents relocated, its houses demolished, the land returned to salt marsh.

CROSSING THE MAWDDACH

Barmouth Bridge is one of the engineering marvels of Victorian Wales, stretching nearly a kilometre across the Mawddach estuary. A combination of timber viaduct and iron swing bridge, it's been carrying trains since 1867. Today, trains still creep across at twenty miles per hour, the structure creaking beneath them. The views from the carriage are spectacular, the estuary widening towards the sea, hills rising on one side, sailboats scattered across the water on the other.

THE STEEPEST STREET IN THE WORLD

As the train continues north, Snowdonia's peaks grow closer. Ahead, visible for miles, is Harlech Castle, perched on a crag high above the village. Built by Edward I in the 1280s as part of his campaign to subdue Wales, it occupies one of the most dramatic sites for a fortress in Britain.

From the station, the climb is punishing. Ffordd Pen Llech has a gradient of more than thirty percent in places and was once certified by Guinness as the steepest street in the world. The title has since passed to a street in New Zealand, though you could have fooled us. Just before the castle gates, the "Shop at the Top" sells cold drinks and ice creams to gasping visitors. We stop for both.

IN THE RAMPARTS

The castle, when you do finally reach it, is magnificent. Massive stone walls enclose a central courtyard, with towers at each corner and battlements commanding views across Tremadog Bay. The site was chosen for its defensive strength. Sheer drops on the seaward side, and on the landward side an approach so steep that attackers would have to climb it under a hail of arrows.

We tuck into Welsh cakes in the tearoom, walk around the castle, then descend carefully to the station. Our train north is delayed, blocked by another service on the single-track line. When it finally arrives, it's packed with schoolchildren heading home, shouting and laughing – a reminder that the Cambrian Coast Line isn't just a tourist attraction but essential infrastructure, linking communities that depend on it.

ON THE EDGE OF SNOWDONIA

That night we stay at a small glamping site near Tremadog, on the edge of Snowdonia National Park, sleeping in a converted western-style wagon with views across to the mountains. In the morning, breakfast is served in a converted cowshed. The owner, Gareth, pours us coffee and points us to the bus to Beddgelert. "Prettiest village in North Wales," he insists, and he's not wrong.

BEDDGELERT

We get off the bus a few stops early and hike the Fisherman's Path, which follows the Glaslyn River through ancient oak woodland to Beddgelert, a village of stone cottages and slate roofs clustered around a bridge where two rivers meet. After exploring the Sygun Copper Mine, we wander the various craft shops and stone bridges before catching the bus to Porthmadog where we walk along the coast to Portmeirion, one of the strangest and most delightful places in Wales.

Designed by architect Clough Williams-Ellis and built over five decades from 1925 to 1976, Portmeirion is an Italianate fantasy brought to life: colourful buildings and clock towers, grottoes and gardens filled with palm trees and hydrangeas, colonnades and fountains, hidden staircases and unexpected viewpoints.

Williams-Ellis wanted to prove that architecture could be exuberant without scarring the landscape, that beauty and conservation could coexist. Walking through Portmeirion in the late afternoon light, it feels both completely artificial and perfectly at home in its surroundings.

CLIMBING THE DUNES

As evening approaches, we take the train to Criccieth, a small town dominated by a ruined castle on a headland. Unlike Harlech and the other fortresses built by Edward I, Criccieth was originally a Welsh castle, built by Llewelyn the Great himself. It was captured by Edward, strengthened, then burned by Owain Glyndŵr's forces in 1404 and never rebuilt.

We climb the dunes behind the station as the sun sinks lower. A train passes below, heading south along the coast, its driver sounding the horn in greeting. The beach is empty save for a few dog walkers. The Llŷn Peninsula stretches westwards, its hills blue in the distance.

TO THE SUMMIT

From Pwllheli, where the Cambrian Coast Line terminates, buses run to Caernarfon and on to Pen-y-Pass, the starting point for several routes up Yr Wyddfa – Mount Snowdon – the highest mountain in Wales.

At 1,085 m (3,560 ft), it's not exceptionally high by European standards, but it is a proper mountain, steep and rocky, often wrapped in cloud, sometimes dangerous in bad weather. Every year, thousands of people underestimate it.

We take the Pyg Track, one of the more popular routes, which climbs steadily past two glacial lakes, Llyn Llydaw and Glaslyn, before ascending a steep scree slope to the summit. The wind buffets us constantly, trying to knock us off balance.

At the top, there's a café and the upper terminus of the Snowdon Mountain Railway, a rack-and-pinion line that's been carrying visitors to the summit since 1896. On clear days, the view stretches across all of north Wales and out to sea. Today the visibility comes and goes. We stop for a tea in the café, watching hikers emerge from the cloud looking dazed and triumphant.

HEADING HOME

The descent via the Miners' Track is gentler, following an old quarrying route to Llyn Llydaw. The slate industry shaped this landscape profoundly, and at its peak in the late nineteenth century, north Wales produced nearly one-third of the world's slate. The industry collapsed in the twentieth century, but its marks remain: spoil heaps, quarries cut into mountainsides, and villages built entirely from the stone pulled from the earth beneath them.

By the time we reach Pen-y-Pass, we're exhausted but satisfied. From Caernarfon, buses connect to Bangor, and from Bangor, trains run direct to London Euston–or Llundain, as the Welsh announcements have it. As the train pulls away and heads east towards England, we're already thinking about when we can come back.

JOURNEY DETAILS

Begins at London Euston
Ends in Pwllheli

Where you'll go
London – Aberystwyth, change at Birmingham or Shrewsbury, 4.5 hours
Aberystwyth – Pwllheli (Cambrian Coast Line), 3.5 hours
Local buses connect to Beddgelert, Caernarfon and Snowdonia

Time needed
At least 4–5 days to explore the region properly. Recommended stops include Aberdyfi, Barmouth, Harlech, Beddgelert, Portmeirion, Criccieth and Caernarfon.

Best time to travel
Summer offers the best weather and longest days, though nowhere in Wales guarantees sunshine. Spring and autumn are quieter and equally beautiful. Winter can be harsh in the mountains but atmospheric along the coast.

Tickets & reservations
Advance tickets from London to Wales can be booked via nationalrail.co.uk. An Interrail Pass works well for flexibility. Local buses are operated by several companies, with timetables available online.

09 SWITZERLAND - ITALY

ZURICH - CATANIA

From the Alps to Mount Etna

Few train journeys end at an active volcano, and fewer still cross an entire country to get there. The trip from Zurich to Catania covers 1,600 km (1,000 mi) of constantly changing scenery, from cool mountain lakes and northern Italian cities to the sun-baked south. You change trains in Milan and Naples, then at the tip of the peninsula board a ferry that carries the whole train across to Sicily, the last service of its kind in Europe. By the time you arrive, Etna is already visible on the horizon.

INTO THE ALPS

We leave Zurich on a bright morning, heading south along the Gotthard line, cutting straight into the Alps. The train slips in and out of tunnels, past sheer rock faces and lakes so still they reflect the mountains like mirrors. The further south we head towards Milan, the softer the landscape becomes. The steep slopes give way to wider valleys, and the light grows warmer. We've made this journey many times, but the scenery still makes us look up.

Our destination for the morning is Lugano, cupped against the hillside above its deep-blue lake. We drop our bags at the hotel and walk down to the waterfront, past the Funicolare Lugano Città, a tiny funicular that has been making the trip since 1886. By the lake, the atmosphere feels distinctly Mediterranean. Palm trees line the promenade. Buildings are painted in soft pinks and yellows. People sit with cappuccinos and watch the world go by. It isn't quite Italy yet, but it certainly feels like it.

CROSSING INTO ITALY

After breakfast, we continue south along the lakeshore, the train hugging the water until we cross the border at Chiasso, near Lake Como. The mountains stay close for a while longer, then gradually fall away as the landscape flattens into the sprawling outskirts of Milan. Before long the city swallows us, and we pull into Milano Centrale.

No matter how many times we arrive here, this station always takes our breath away. Opened in 1931, it's Europe's largest by volume, but more marble palace than railway terminus. The ceilings soar overhead, the walls decorated with frescoes and mosaics. The façade is monumental, designed to awe. Architect Ulisse Stacchini took inspiration from Union Station in Washington, D.C., though many believe he surpassed it in grandeur. Frank Lloyd Wright apparently called it the most beautiful station in the world. Standing in the main hall, surrounded by all that marble and light, we're not about to argue.

THE NIGHT TRAIN SOUTH

Milano Centrale is also where one of Europe's great overnight journeys begins. The Intercity Notte to Sicily takes nearly twenty hours, winding through the mountains to Genoa, then hugging the coast all the way down the peninsula before boarding a ferry to cross to the island. There's no dining car, so you bring your own food and settle in for the night.

We've taken this train before, and there's something magical about it. Falling asleep as the lights of small towns flicker past, waking to the sea outside your window, and then the crossing itself, the train rolling onto the ferry as dawn breaks over the strait. Every train to Sicily still makes this crossing by ship. It's the last rail ferry in Europe, and it's an experience few rail journeys can match.

THE FAST WAY TO NAPLES

This time, though, we travel by day, as the views are simply too good to miss. In Milan, we board the Frecciarossa for Naples, a sleek red high-speed train that covers the 800 km (500 mi) in just four and a half hours, calling only at Bologna, Florence and Rome. Conductors usher us on board, the doors close with a hiss, and within minutes we're gliding south.

The Frecciarossa is built for comfort: wide seats, quiet carriages, Wi-Fi that actually works. An attendant comes through with a trolley and an espresso machine, and soon the carriage smells of fresh coffee. We order two cups and watch central Italy fly past. The red rooftops of Bologna, the hills of Tuscany, the outskirts of Rome. When Vesuvius finally rises out of the haze, we're already close to our stop for the night.

NAPLES

Naples, when we step off the train, feels intense and irresistible. Even underground, the city makes an impression, having turned some of its a metro stations into art installations. Toledo, with its blue mosaics, is regularly called one of the most beautiful stations in the world – and Università, a few stops away, bursts with fluorescent colours. They're an unexpected and very welcome detour. Above ground, the city feels a world apart. Scooters dart through narrow streets, laundry hangs from weathered balconies, and baroque churches appear around almost every corner. The bay glitters in the distance, Vesuvius looming behind it. We could spend a week here and barely scratch the surface.

And then there's the pizza. Naples is where it was invented, and Antica Pizzeria Port'Alba claims

to be the oldest pizzeria in the world, serving customers since 1738. Inside, the air smells of ripe tomatoes and woodsmoke. The menu runs to more than forty varieties, and a photo on the wall shows the owner posing with Gordon Ramsay.

MOUNT VESUVIUS

The volcano dominates Naples and you see it from almost everywhere, beautiful and slightly menacing. In AD 79, it buried Pompeii and Herculaneum in a single catastrophic day. Today, vineyards cover its slopes, thriving in the rich volcanic soil. That mix of danger and life has drawn visitors for centuries. Travellers on the Grand Tour made a climb to the summit a rite of passage, and the route is still popular today. The mountain hasn't erupted since 1944, but it remains active, and at the top you can peer into the crater and see wisps of steam escape from the rocks. The easiest way to explore is on the Circumvesuviana, an old local train that rattles around the base of the volcano. From Naples, it heads towards Sorrento, stopping at Ercolano and Pompei along the way with easy access to both ancient sites. The views from the windows are pure Naples: lemon groves, washing lines, glimpses of the bay.

DOWN THE COAST

Early the next morning, we board an Intercity bound for Taormina. Seven hours of travel lie ahead, our first night in Sicily at the other end. From Salerno, the train follows the coast. The Tyrrhenian Sea stretches out to the right, blue and glittering. We pass the national parks of Cilento and Pollino, wild and green, then continue south through Calabria as the landscape grows drier.

Our train barely stops, but regional services run the same route more slowly if you want to explore along the way.

BOARDING THE FERRY

At Villa San Giovanni, near the toe of Italy, we reach the Strait of Messina. The train edges forward, stops, reverses, inches forward again, until the carriages are aligned to roll into the hull of a waiting ferry. The crossing to Messina takes about half an hour, and we head up to the deck and watch Sicily approach, Etna in the distance, a thin line of smoke rising from its summit. This is Europe's last train ferry. Bridge plans have come and gone for decades, but for now the ships keep running.

A JEWEL ON THE EAST COAST

From Messina, we continue down the eastern coast, eventually passing Isola Bella, a tiny island in a turquoise bay that looks almost too beautiful to be real. If it seems familiar, you might have seen it in *The White Lotus*. We get off at Taormina-Giardini, a handsome Art Nouveau station with ornate ceilings and a setting right on the water. The town of Taormina sits 200 m (656 ft) above on the hillside, reached by a winding bus ride that takes about fifteen minutes. The highlight is the Teatro Greco, an ancient amphitheatre with a view that takes in the coast, the sea, and Etna all at once. We arrive in the late afternoon and stay until the light fades.

CATANIA

The next day, we take a slow train further south. Catania is an hour down the coast, and the journey is beautiful – the sea on one side, the volcano on the other. The city, when we arrive, has a character all its own. The buildings are made of black lava stone, giving the streets a dark, dramatic look. Markets spill out onto the pavements. Vendors sell espresso from carts. Fishmongers shout out the day's catch. The noise and energy are infectious. Catania has been buried by Etna more than once. Eruptions in 1169 and 1669 destroyed entire neighbourhoods. Each time, the city rebuilt itself from the same black stone that had ruined it. You see it everywhere – lava blocks in the walls, basalt paving the streets. The volcano looms over the rooftops, a reminder that none of this is permanent. And yet the city feels stubbornly alive.

AROUND THE VOLCANO

The following morning, we board the Ferrovia Circumetnea, a narrow-gauge railway that circles almost entirely around Etna. Built in the late nineteenth century to carry agricultural produce from the mountain villages down to the port, it still runs today, though lava flows have forced parts of the track to be moved over the years. The trains are old Fiat railcars from the 1950s, and riding them

feels like travelling back in time. We leave Catania and climb into a landscape of prickly pears and citrus orchards, with solidified lava fields higher up. Etna is always there, sometimes just a slope filling the window, sometimes the whole mountain. After Bronte, famous for the pistachios that have grown here since the Arabs arrived in the ninth century, we reach the line's highest point at Rocca Calanna, nearly 1,000 m (3,280 ft) up. Then we descend to Randazzo, a medieval town built from black volcanic stone. The buildings, the churches, the narrow lanes – everything looks carved from the same dark rock. We stop for wine at Enoteca Il Buongustaio dell'Etna, trying bottles made from grapes grown on the volcano's slopes. An Etna Rosso, an Etna Bianco, a Carricante that tastes of citrus and minerals. Wine doesn't get more local than this.

WALKING ON ETNA

Our last day takes us up Etna itself. A guide drives us to Piano Provenzana, 1,800 m (5,900 ft) up, and from there we walk out across the lava fields. The landscape is stark and strange. Black rock, twisted formations, caves where ancient flows once ran. In places, steam rises from cracks in the ground. We get back to Catania as the sun is setting, tired and happy, and stop at a street stall for arancini, crispy fried rice balls, golden and hot. We eat them standing up, watching the last light catch the buildings. The whole trip has been worth it. The Alps, the lakes, the crossing to Sicily. But this final day on the volcano is the one we'll remember longest.

JOURNEY DETAILS

Begins at Zurich Hauptbahnhof, Switzerland
Ends at Catania Centrale, Italy

Where you'll go
Zurich is a major rail hub, easily reached by direct trains from Paris, Frankfurt, Munich, Berlin, Vienna and Milan.

Zurich – Lugano, 2 hours
Lugano – Naples, change in Milan, 6.5 hours
Naples – Taormina, 7 hours
Taormina – Catania, 1 hour
Circumetnea: Catania Borgo – Randazzo, 2 hours

Time needed
At least one week, ideally two.

When to travel
Apart from the crowds in July and August, we recommend avoiding summer completely due to the high temperatures.

Tickets & reservations
An Interrail Pass for 7–10 days covers almost the entire route. In Italy, additional seat reservations are required for the high speed & Intercity trains. The Circumetnea needs a separate ticket.

10 AUSTRIA - SLOVAKIA

VIENNA - KOŠICE

Heading East into Slovakia

When we booked tickets to Košice, we knew embarrassingly little about Slovakia. The eastbound train from Vienna has none of the glamour of Europe's classic rail routes and rarely makes it onto bucket lists. But it should. The route crosses almost the entire country, winding through vineyards and castle towns into the Carpathians, surprising us at every turn: Europe's last mountain sherpas hauling supplies by hand, medieval tales of a blood-bathing countess, and landscapes most travellers never see.

A TASTE OF VIENNA

With an hour to spare before our train, we wander over to Café Goldegg, a five-minute walk from Vienna Hauptbahnhof. From outside it looks unassuming, but step through the doors and you're transported to the turn of the last century: green velvet upholstery, brass chandeliers, elegant wood panelling, even a couple of billiard tables.

Opened in 1910, the café once teemed with railway workers enjoying their morning coffee. Later it became a meeting place for underground trade unionists and resistance fighters during the Second World War. We order a melange, an Austrian speciality a bit like a cappuccino, and watch the morning light stream through the tall windows.

ENTERING SLOVAKIA

Trains to Bratislava leave every hour, but we briefly consider taking the Twin City Liner instead, a fast catamaran that skims along the Danube in seventy minutes, passing the ruins of Devín Castle perched perilously on a clifftop. But we're here for the trains, so we board our carriage and settle in for the hour-long ride.

The landscape stays flat as we roll east through farmland and quiet villages. After Marchegg, we cross the River Morava and officially enter Slovakia. Through the window, the floodplains look peaceful. It's hard to imagine that a few decades ago, this same ground bristled with barbed wire, watchtowers and landmines marking the Iron Curtain.

BRATISLAVA'S HIDDEN CHARMS

Bratislava takes a moment to win you over. The first impression is traffic and concrete, but walk into the old town and everything changes: narrow cobbled lanes, hidden courtyards, grand Habsburg-era palaces painted in fading pastels. From there, it's a twenty-minute walk uphill to Bratislava Castle, which sits 85 m (280 ft) above the Danube. Hungarian kings once stored their crown jewels here. Now it offers panoramic views over the city's rooftops, the river curving west towards Vienna.

Below the castle walls, we find Viecha pod hradom, a tiny wine bar tucked into a cellar. The owner pours us a Slovak cabernet sauvignon from the Južnoslovenská region in the south. "People don't expect good wine from here," he says. "Austria gets the reputation. We get the grapes." He's right, of course, and it's surprisingly good, with more body than we expected. Appetites whetted, we head to Café Verne and order bryndzové halušky, soft potato dumplings smothered in tangy sheep's cheese, washing it down with a Kofola, Slovakia's answer to Coca-Cola.

CASTLES AND VINEYARDS

Next morning, tram 1 carries us to Bratislava's main station, a tired concrete structure that's seen better days. As we step off, a recorded voice thanks us for choosing eco-friendly public transport. Above the main hall, there's a faded but striking Communist-era mural, showing workers under a red banner, doves flying overhead. We walk beneath it and board the regional train to Trenčín.

The city drops away quickly. Grey apartment blocks give way to vineyards, then small villages with painted houses and church spires. We're skirting the Malé Karpaty now – the Little Carpathians – forested hills on Slovakia's western edge. Every so often a castle appears, silhouetted against the spring sky. Just before Trenčín, we cross the Váh, Slovakia's longest river, which rises in the Tatras and flows 400 km (250 mi) south to meet the Danube.

THE BLOOD COUNTESS

Trenčín charms us before we even step off the train, its castle rising steeply above the town. We walk through a small park to Mierové námestie, the main square, ringed with Baroque buildings and outdoor cafés doing brisk business in the midday sun.

Inside the castle, among the displays of armour and Renaissance furniture, we learn about Countess Elisabeth Báthory, the "Blood Countess," who ruled nearby estates in the early 1600s. She never lived in this castle, though her portrait hangs on one of the walls. Legend says she killed hundreds of young women, bathing in their blood to preserve her youth. The truth is far murkier, tangled up in politics and rival nobles, but the stories have endured. Trenčín, incidentally, will be a Europe-

an Capital of Culture in 2026, but whether the countess earns a mention remains to be seen.

INTO THE MOUNTAINS

Beyond Trenčín, the train hugs the Váh through increasingly narrow valleys, following the edge of Veľká Fatra, one of Slovakia's nine national parks – almost entirely forested, riddled with caves, and popular with hikers.

After Kraľovany, the landscape shifts. The forests grow denser, the river faster. For a stretch, it feels oddly Scandinavian, all pine trees and rushing water. Then we roll into Ružomberok, where the station is painted imperial blue, its narrow platforms preserved from the Kaiserzeit, when this was Habsburg land.

Ahead, the horizon fills with mountains. The Carpathians rise in long, forested ridges – the High Tatras and Low Tatras, sparsely populated, still patched with snow in early May. The highest peak, Gerlachovský štít, reaches 2,655 m (8,710 ft).

POPRAD AND ITS VILLAGES

Poprad's station is pure Brutalism, with concrete slabs and sharp angles, but right beside it stands the Hotel Európa, an Art Deco beauty from 1898 that's been welcoming travellers for over a century. We walk to the main square, slightly shabby but charming, and visit the Church of St Egidius. Inside, beneath a thirteenth-century bell tower, medieval frescoes still adorn the walls, a few even depicting the Tatras.

Just outside Poprad lies Spišská Sobota, a village so well-preserved it feels like a film set. Once independent, now technically part of the city, it centres on a long square lined with Gothic, Renaissance and Baroque houses, their façades painted in yellows, blues and reds. On special days, the square fills with folk musicians and vendors selling handicrafts. You can easily imagine centuries of traders pausing here before pushing on into the mountains.

THE MOUNTAIN RAILWAY

The next morning, we rise early to catch the Tatra Electric Railway, a narrow-gauge line that has linked the mountain towns here since 1908. Red-and-white carriages hum quietly from Poprad-Tatry to Štrbské Pleso, stopping at thirteen stations, some barely more than a wooden shelter and a dirt path disappearing into the trees. The Tatras rise ahead, jagged and dramatic. At Starý Smokovec, we switch to a branch line heading to Tatranská Lomnica, then board a cable car that climbs to Skalnaté Pleso, a high mountain lake at one of Slovakia's windiest spots. Even in May, the air bites.

WALKING WITH WILDLIFE

The Tatras boast more than 600 km (370 mi) of marked trails. We follow part of the Tatranská magistrála, a long-distance path that traces the range's southern flank just above the tree line. On one side, the main peaks, grey rock and white snow. On the other, a broad valley stretching towards the Low Tatras, green and peaceful. Bears still live in these forests, as do wolves. We don't see either, but we do spot two golden eagles drifting overhead. The trail leads past mountain lakes, waterfalls and a series of old stone huts, including Rainer's Chalet from 1863 and Skalnatá Chalet, where signs warn hikers that bears occasionally wander too close. One famously managed to get into the hut keeper's bedroom a few years back, although these days, hungry bears are more likely to raid village rubbish bins.

THE LAST PORTERS

Descending towards Hrebienok, we see him: an older man bent beneath a tall wooden frame stacked with crates, moving slowly but steadily uphill. He's a horský šerpa, a mountain porter, one of the last of his kind in Europe. The tradition dates to the 1800s, when the first hiking trails and mountain shelters were built. Porters hauled everything by hand: food, fuel, building materials. Many still carry over 100 kg (220 lbs) at a time.

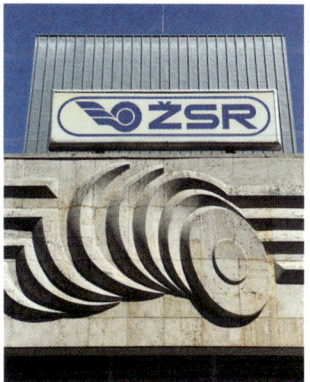

The most famous was Ladislav Kulanga, who once shouldered 211 kg (465 lbs) in a single load, a record that still stands. He worked for more than fifty years until an accident in 2020 claimed his life. His story appears in *Freedom Under Load*, a documentary that captures both the physical toll and the quiet pride of the work.

Back in Smokovec, we toast the porters with cold Zlatý Bažant beer on the terrace of Koliba Kamzík, a wooden mountain restaurant.

KOŠICE AT LAST

From Poprad, the train continues east. The mountains fall behind. Fields of yellow rapeseed stretch under a cloudless sky. Between small towns, we pass lakes, farmhouses, and Communist-era apartment blocks. At every rural stop, the stationmaster waves us off with a red paddle, a tradition that has somehow survived modernisation.

Near the Hungarian border, Košice has long stood at a crossroads. Its main street, Hlavná ulica, bursts with colour with cafés spilling onto the pavement and buskers playing under the trees. The car-free centre is the result of a bold move by former mayor Rudolf Schuster in 1995. People thought he was mad, but he later went on to become president.

A narrow stream runs down the middle of the street, where locals cool their feet in summer. Nearby, a "singing fountain" sends jets of water into the air dancing to music. After nearly a week of trains, castles, and mountains, we're content to sit beneath a linden tree and watch Košice move at its own unhurried pace.

JOURNEY DETAILS

Begins at Vienna Hauptbahnhof, Austria
Ends at Košice, Slovakia

Where you'll go
Vienna – Bratislava, 1 hour
Bratislava – Trenčín, 1.5 hours
Trenčín – Poprad, 3 hours
Poprad – Košice, 1.5 hours
Košice – Bratislava, 5 hours

Tatra Electric Railway:
Poprad – Štrbské Pleso, 1 hour
Štrbské Pleso – Tatranská Lomnica, change at Starý Smokovec, 1 hour

Time needed
This journey can comfortably be done in seven days. At weekends, volunteers run heritage trains from Poprad and Starý Smokovec along the foothills of the High Tatras. You can ride the beautifully restored Kométa (1913) or the classic Trojča (1969), both slow, nostalgic trains that suit the region perfectly. Details at tatranskaelektricka.sk.

Tickets & reservations
We used a 7-day Interrail/Eurail Global Pass (valid for one month), including the onward journey to Vienna, though buying individual tickets may be cheaper. Check zssk.sk for fares. A day ticket for the Tatra Electric Railway from Poprad costs around €4.

HANNOVER – HARZ MOUNTAINS

Steam Trains and Witches

For forty years, the Brocken was a ghost. Northern Germany's highest peak, a place where Goethe set his witches' gathering and the Brothers Grimm collected their darkest tales, sat behind barbed wire, home to a Soviet listening post and off-limits to everyone else. The steam trains still ran partway up the mountain, but the summit was silent.

Today, more than a million passengers a year ride those same trains to the top. The Harzer Schmalspurbahnen (HSB) form Germany's largest narrow-gauge network, with 140 km (87 mi) of track winding through the Harz Mountains. In winter, it looks like something out of a fairy tale: snow-dusted forests, medieval castles, white expanses and crisp mountain air.

THROUGH THE FOOTHILLS

We begin in Hannover, a couple of hours north of the mountains. If you have time, the baroque Herrenhausen Gardens are worth a morning-vast formal lawns, fountains, hedge mazes and one of Europe's great royal parks, shaped largely by Sophia of Hanover, whose son would later become George I of Great Britain. From the main station, an hourly regional train heads south into the Harz foothills. The blue-and-yellow Erixx service rolls through flat farmland, the land rising gently as we approach Hildesheim.

Hildesheim itself is worth a quick detour. Two of its churches are UNESCO World Heritage Sites, and climbing the 364 steps of St Andrew's tower rewards you with views over a marketplace ringed by half-timbered houses so perfectly preserved they look like toys. On clear days, you can even spot the Brocken from here, though today, it's snowing. Back on the train, we continue south to Goslar. Snow thickens along the tracks, and the forests close in.

GOSLAR

Goslar is one of northern Germany's most beautiful towns. For centuries, it served as a resting point for travellers braving the dense Harz forests. Mining brought enormous wealth during the Middle Ages, and it shows in the grand merchants' houses surrounding the marketplace. The Siemenshaus, built in 1693 by the family who would later found the industrial giant, is among the finest. Unlike much of the region, the old town survived the war intact. Today it's a UNESCO-listed labyrinth of narrow streets and more than 1,500 half-timbered buildings, their beams dark with age. We wander for an hour, then catch the train to Wernigerode, half an hour east.

WERNIGERODE

Just after we leave, we pass through Vienenburg, a tiny station with a surprising distinction. Opened in 1840, it's the oldest still in operation in Germany today, and once marked the final stop before the East–West border. Kaiser Wilhelm I rested here in the station's lavish Emperor's Hall during an 1875 visit. Today it houses a café, a library and a small railway museum. Wernigerode makes an ideal base for exploring the Harz. Its old town is a patchwork of brightly painted houses that look even more magical under fresh snow. The Gothic town hall, with its twin pointed towers, dominates the central square, and is often described as one of the most beautiful in Europe. The town has even

appeared in films, including *The Monuments Men*. Above the rooftops sits Wernigerode Castle, a mix of medieval fortifications and 19th-century reconstruction, with around fifty rooms open to visitors, including a rather chilling torture chamber displaying medieval instruments of punishment.

Even if you skip the interior, the views from the terrace stretch across the Harz to the Brocken and are well worth the climb. Wernigerode also has a cluster of small, eclectic museums covering everything from East German design to aviation. And rail fans also shouldn't miss the historic HSB workshop, housed in an industrial hall dating back to 1926, where locomotives and carriages are still rebuilt and repaired by hand.

RAILWAY ROMANCE

The steam train to the Brocken takes around an hour and forty minutes, and at the HSB station beside Wernigerode Hauptbahnhof, you can still buy your traditional cardboard Edmondson ticket. The red-and-white carriages, pulled by a coal-fired locomotive, chug past back gardens and four small stations before the track begins its steep ascent. The train twists through the Drängetal Valley, passes the route's only tunnel, and reaches Drei Annen Hohne, where the snow deepens and the wind sharpens.

The journey itself feels wonderfully timeless. The smell of coal, the hiss of steam, the conductor punching holes in our ticket. With the train averaging just 25 km/h (15 mph), you can even

step out onto the open balcony at the end of the carriage and let the cold mountain air sting your face.

THE SUMMIT

The Brocken is bare and exposed, its climate closer to Iceland or the Alps than to the lowlands an hour below. When we arrive, dense fog swirls around the platform and gusts of wind nearly knock us sideways. Winter is when the mountain feels most atmospheric. Snow covers the summit for roughly 178 days a year, and it often sits above the clouds. When the fog lifts, the views reach for miles. But conditions can be brutal. Wind chill has been recorded at -42°C (-44°F), so dress accordingly. We warm up in the Brockenhaus visitor centre, then duck into the Hexenflug café for hot chocolate and watch the next train arrive through the mist.

Sadly, there's a melancholy side to the Brocken too. Much of the surrounding forest has died in recent years, weakened by drought, storms and bark beetle infestations, all linked to a changing climate. Yet even stripped of its trees, the mountain feels apart from the world. For hikers, the 97-kilometre (60 mi) Harzer-Hexen-Stieg — the Witches' Trail, once voted Germany's most beautiful long-distance path — is unforgettable, especially sections along the old East–West border. Walk through the winter forest and you'll find rusting watchtowers still standing where the border once ran. It's beautiful, but all rather haunting.

JOURNEY DETAILS

Begins at Hannover Hauptbahnhof
Ends at Wernigerode Hauptbahnhof

Where you'll go
Hannover has direct connections to Amsterdam, Berlin, Hamburg and Munich.

Hannover – Goslar, 1 hour
Goslar – Wernigerode, 30 min
Wernigerode – Brocken, 1 hour 45 min

Time needed
Ideally 3 to 5 days. This trip can be done in a long weekend.

Best time to travel
The Harz Mountains are appealing in any season, but the Brocken is at its most mysterious in winter.

Tickets & reservations
In Germany, the Deutschland-Ticket offers excellent value, providing unlimited travel on public transport, including all the regional trains mentioned. The HSB steam trains are included, except for the section between Drei Annen Hohne and the Brocken. The Deutschland-Ticket is sold as a monthly subscription, but you can purchase it for just one month. Alternatively, use an Interrail / Eurail One Country Pass for Germany, also valid for all high-speed trains, or get the Quer-durchs-Land-Ticket at bahn.de.

Up-to-date information on departure times and tickets is available at hsb-wr.de. Trains run daily, but there are different timetables in winter and summer.

12   GERMANY — AUSTRIA — SLOVENIA - CROATIA

FRANKFURT - SPLIT

Over the Alps to the Adriatic

Taking the train from Frankfurt to Split may not be the fastest way to reach the Croatian coast, nor the most obvious. But it is one of the more exciting. It crosses the Austrian Alps, passes through Slovenia, and then follows a single-track line across the Croatian interior. Over the course of a day, the journey carries us from mountains and river valleys, through vineyards and war-scarred towns, to the glittering Adriatic, where the rails finally meet the sea.

THROUGH THE ALPS

The Adriatic feels a long way off as we board the high-speed ICE train in Frankfurt. Zagreb lies twelve and a half hours to the south, with Split another six beyond that. The journey begins gently, passing rolling hills and vineyards, with early highlights such as Ulm's church tower – until recently the tallest in the world – rising clearly into view from the train window. After Munich, however, everything shifts. The hills grow into mountains, and by the time we cross into Austria at Salzburg, the scenery demands our full attention.

From the dining car, we watch the turquoise Salzach river run alongside the tracks while steep mountains rise on the other side. The train cuts

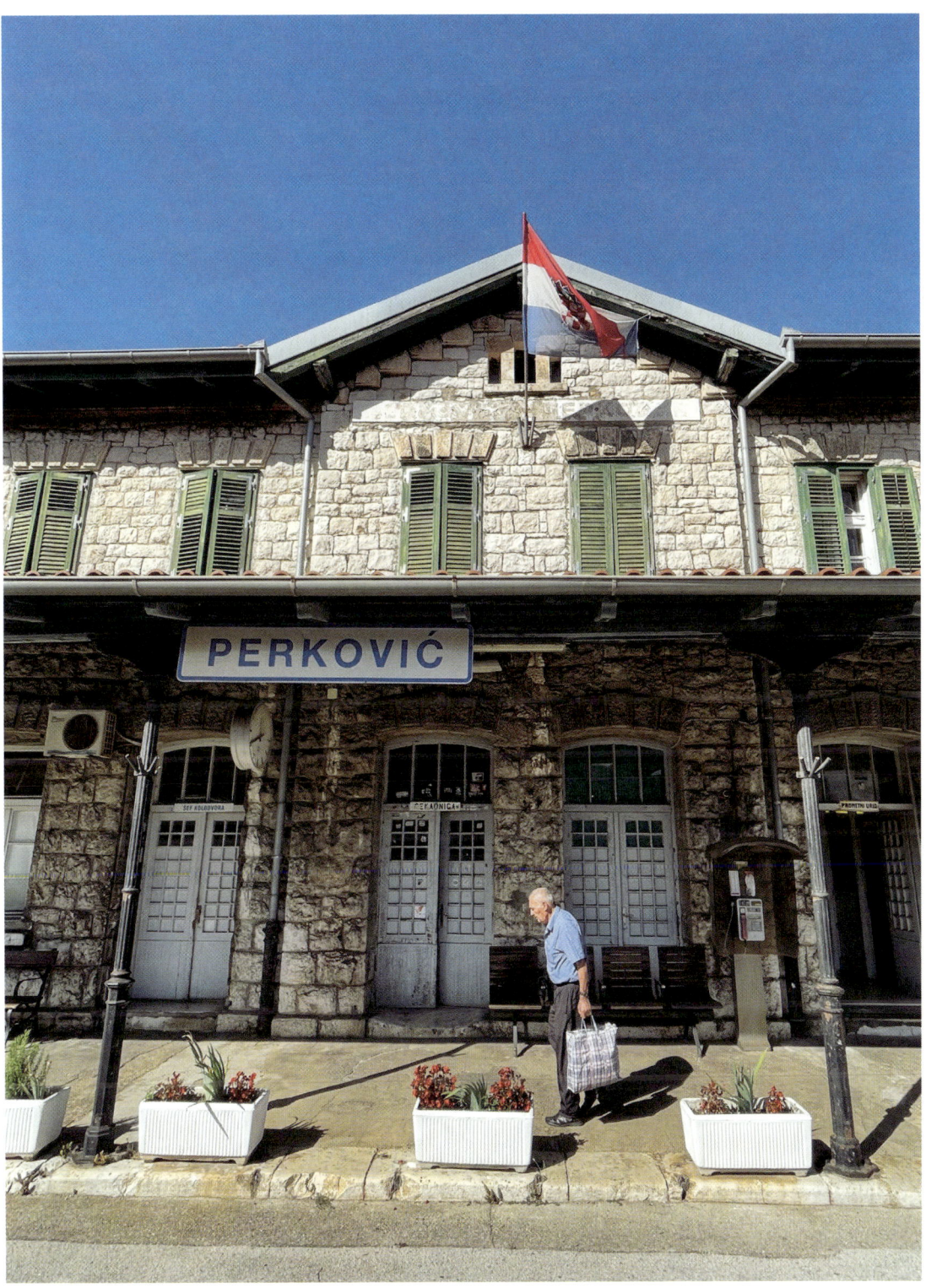

through valleys, past Alpine villages with church spires and cable cars, and castles on the hilltops. It's October, but the sun is bright and the hillsides are still green.

At Villach, near the Slovenian border, we board the next train, which carries us through Slovenia, following the Sava River as it tumbles through forested valleys. Small villages appear along the water, occasionally a grand house tucked between the trees. We skip Ljubljana this time, though Lake Bled is just a short detour from Lesce-Bled station if you want to stop.

ZAGREB

We get to Zagreb that evening. The city sits between the Sava River and the Medvednica mountains, and compared to the Croatian coast, it feels refreshingly unhurried and tourist-free. Most visitors head straight for Split or Dubrovnik, but that's their loss.

The main station, Glavni Kolodvor, was opened in 1892 by Emperor Franz Joseph I, back when Croatia was part of the Austro-Hungarian Empire, and the occasion was considered important enough to schedule for the emperor's birthday. The building still has a faded imperial grandeur about it. Directly opposite stands the Hotel Esplanade, built in 1925 to accommodate passengers on the Orient Express, which passed through Zagreb on its way from Paris to Istanbul. Agatha Christie stayed here in the 1930s, supposedly finding inspiration for Murder on the Orient Express.

Zagreb itself is easy to like. It's small enough to explore on foot, with a handsome old town and a network of blue trams rattling through the streets. One day is enough to get a feel for the place, although two would be better.

DOWN THROUGH CROATIA

The next morning, we board the train to Split. As almost every Croatian we meet is quick to point out, Croatia is not a train country. The network is limited, mostly single-track, and run by ageing diesel locomotives. Outside Zagreb, the railways have been neglected for decades. The line to Split, which dates back more than a century, passes through some of the most beautiful and empty landscape in the country. It also passes through territory that saw heavy fighting in the 1990s. Villages were abandoned, infrastructure destroyed, and the rebuilding has been slow. The tracks are open again now, but the scars remain. None of this deters us, though. If anything, it adds to the journey's sense of adventure.

THE LONG WAY SOUTH

Leaving the city, we cross the Sava and climb into the hills, the route winding through rural Croatia, rising for views across wide valleys, then dropping into dense forest where the only signs of life are occasional farmhouses with chickens in the garden. Roadside stalls sell honey and pumpkins. The train takes sharp curves and crosses viaducts that seem surprisingly high for such a quiet line.

The stations along the way vary wildly. Some serve actual villages, others amount to nothing more than a patch of gravel beside the tracks, with no platform and no visible reason to stop. A few retain proper station buildings staffed by officials in old-fashioned uniforms, complete with peaked caps and whistles.

The landscape through the Dinaric Alps is a mix of pine forest, open fields and rough, empty country. Here and there, we pass houses that were destroyed in the war and never rebuilt. The driver sounds the horn frequently, sometimes at level crossings, sometimes seemingly for no reason at all. It feels like travelling through a place the rest of Europe has forgotten.

ŠIBENIK

At Perković, you can change to an even smaller train for the coastal town of Šibenik. It's less famous than Split or Dubrovnik, but just as beautiful and far less crowded. King Edward VIII and Wallis Simpson arrived here by train in August 1936, at the start of their scandalous Adriatic cruise. The station hasn't changed much since. The old town is one of the largest Venetian settlements on the Adriatic, with narrow stone streets and several surviving forts. The highlight is the Cathedral of St James, a UNESCO World Heritage Site built entirely from white stone quarried on the island of Brač, without any brick, iron, wood, or cement. Nothing quite like it exists anywhere else in Europe.

ARRIVAL IN SPLIT

Back on the main line, the final stretch to Split is the most beautiful of all. The train winds through vineyards and olive groves, past apple orchards and small streams. Then, in the last half hour, the sea appears. On one side, the Adriatic glitters in the afternoon light, with vines and cypress trees in the foreground. On the other, mountains rise steeply. Split appears below us, the bell tower of St Domnius Cathedral growing larger as we descend into the city.

The station sits right by the harbour, which makes for a dramatic arrival. The building itself is small and slightly shabby, a reminder that Croatian railways aren't expecting a renaissance anytime soon. But it doesn't matter. We step off the train into warm salt air, the old town a few minutes' walk away, ferries waiting at the quay for the islands beyond.

JOURNEY DETAILS

Begins at Frankfurt Hauptbahnhof, Germany
Ends at Split, Croatia

Where you'll go
Frankfurt – Zagreb, change in Villach, 12.5 hours
Zagreb – Šibenik, change in Perković, 6 hours
Šibenik – Split, change in Perković, 1.5 hours
Zagreb – Split, 6.5 hours

Time needed
At least a week is recommended to explore along the way. Stops worth considering are Ljubljana, Lake Bled, Zagreb, Šibenik, Krka National Park, Hvar, and of course Split.

Tickets & reservations
We used a 7-day Interrail Pass (valid within one month). No seat reservations are required, although trains can be very busy during high season, so a reservation is recommended. These can't currently be made online, so you'll need to visit the ticket office in Zagreb. As Croatian train fares are relatively inexpensive, an Interrail Pass may not be the most economical option for this part of the journey.

13 SWITZERLAND

BERN - JUNGFRAUJOCH

Above the Clouds at Jungfraujoch

Even in summer, the view from the Jungfraujoch is all white. Snow lies deep around the station and the Alps' largest glacier stretches into the distance. This is the highest railway station in Europe, reached by a train that climbs through the mountain itself, stopping at stations carved into the rock where windows open onto a frozen world.

Just before the train pulls into Bern, it crosses a bridge over the River Aare and the old town comes into view, terracotta rooftops clustered beneath the spire of Bern Minster with the Alps rising pale and sharp behind. As arrivals go, it's pretty hard to beat.

For a capital city, Bern feels surprisingly intimate. The UNESCO-listed centre is a network of medieval streets with 6 km (3.5 mi) of covered arcades, which protect you from the rain or snow. You can wander the whole place without ever getting wet. There's also an unexpected link to scientific history hidden in these quiet streets. In the early 1900s, Albert Einstein lived in a small flat on Kramgasse while working at the patent office, and it was here that he developed his theory of relativity. Today his apartment is open to visitors.

GATEWAY TO THE ALPS

From Bern, the train to Thun takes less than half an hour. The town grew rapidly after the railway arrived in 1859 and within a few years, no fewer than fourteen grand hotels had sprung up along the lake, catering to Europeans eager to experience the Alps without giving up comfort. When the line was later extended to Interlaken, the crowds thinned here, but traces of that Belle Époque glamour remain.

The old town is particularly lovely with overhanging roofs and painted shopfronts. Above it all stands Thun Castle, its white towers visible long before you reach the town. The climb up is steep but worth every step, and from the ramparts, Lake Thun stretches out, backed by the snowy silhouettes of the Eiger, Mönch and Jungfrau mountains. It's our first real glimpse of the high Alps.

ALONG LAKE THUN

Our train follows Lake Thun's southern shore for almost half an hour, mist hovering over the water, the mountains drifting in and out of cloud. In Switzerland, even the most routine local train feels like a scenic trip you ought to be paying a premium for.

At Interlaken Ost, the region's main transport hub, another of our favourite panoramic routes begins, the GoldenPass Express to Montreux and the vineyards of Lake Geneva. But that will have to wait. Today, the high Alps are calling.

THE CLIMB BEGINS

The classic route to the Jungfraujoch has several stages: Interlaken to Lauterbrunnen or Grindelwald; then onward to Kleine Scheidegg; then a short hop to Eigergletscher; and finally the cogwheel train through the mountain itself. It takes a little over two hours. There is a faster way to the top, the Eiger Express cable car from Grindelwald Terminal, but we're here for the trains, so we settle in for the ride.

From Grindelwald, the train ascends towards Kleine Scheidegg with ever more dramatic views of the Eiger's north face, a sheer 1,800-metre (5,900-ft) wall of rock and ice, notorious amongst climbers. The routes are long, dangerous and prone to avalanches and rockfall, and more than seventy climbers have died attempting them. Seeing the face up close, from the safety of our warm carriage, is humbling.

BUILDING THE IMPOSSIBLE

The Eiger, Mönch, and Jungfrau stand in a row like giants, captivating everyone from poets to engineers. In the late 19th century, ambitious plans for a mountain railway had circulated for years, and in 1896 work finally began on what was meant to be the easy part, a modest two-kilometre (1.2-mile) stretch between Kleine Scheidegg and Eigergletscher that still took over two years to complete. When the first train finally passed through the completed tunnel in 1912, the world called it an engineering miracle and more than a century later, it still feels like one.

THROUGH THE MOUNTAIN

At Kleine Scheidegg, trains from Grindelwald and Lauterbrunnen meet. From the platform, the red Jungfraubahn trains look tiny against the vast snowfields. We see some skiers carving lines down

the slopes, the Eiger rising above them, dark and immense.

From Eigergletscher, the train enters the tunnel and we begin the steepest part of the climb in darkness. Somewhere inside the mountain we cross a watershed: meltwater on one side flows south to the Mediterranean; on the other it heads north through the Aare and Rhine to the North Sea. Halfway up, the train pauses at Eismeer, or "Sea of Ice," where a window has been cut through the mountainside, offering a view of snow and stone stretching into the distance. It's a strange feeling, standing inside the mountain and looking out at all that frozen space.

THE ROOF OF EUROPE

The Jungfraujoch sits on the narrow saddle between the Mönch and Jungfrau peaks and at 3,454 m (11,332 ft) it holds the title of the highest railway station in Europe.

From the viewing platform, the panorama is breathtaking. To the south, 4,000-metre (13,000 ft) peaks march towards Italy. To the north, on an exceptionally clear day, you can see as far as the Vosges Mountains in France. Below us lies the Aletsch Glacier, 22 km (13.6 mi) long and nearly a kilometre deep, a slow-moving river of ice that dominates the landscape. But even this giant is shrinking. Every year it retreats a little further, and scientists estimate it could lose half its volume by the end of the century. A sobering reminder that even seemingly eternal landscapes are fragile.

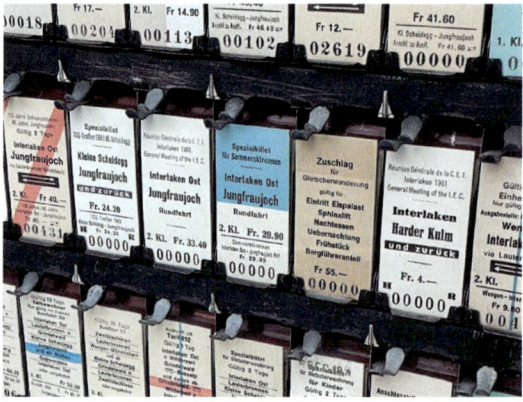

Today, though, the weather is flawless. The sun is brilliant, the air needle-sharp. Even if clouds roll in, there's plenty to explore: exhibitions about the railway's construction and the Alpine environment, tunnels through the ice, and the Ice Palace, a network of chambers and sculptures carved into the glacier by mountain guides in the 1930s.

For the journey back, we follow the line through Lauterbrunnen, and as the train winds down the mountainside, the Valley of 72 Waterfalls opens up to our left. In summer, meltwater can pour over the cliffs at nearly 20,000 litres per second, but even now, in the cooler months, several waterfalls still plunge down the rock face, a final reminder of the power of the mountains we've just left behind.

JOURNEY DETAILS

Begins at Bern
Ends at Jungfraujoch

Where you'll go
Bern is easily reached from Zurich in one hour.
Bern – Thun, 15 min
Thun – Interlaken Ost, 30 min
Interlaken Ost – Jungfraujoch, change at Grindelwald and Kleine Scheidegg, 2 hours

Taking the Eiger Express cable car from Grindelwald Terminal directly to Eigergletscher saves about 30 minutes.

Time needed
This trip can be done in one day, but we recommend staying much longer in the Berner Oberland and, for example, taking the Golden Pass Express (also valid with Interrail/Eurail Pass without reservation) all the way to Lake Geneva.

When to travel
If you want to see snow, you can come year-round. In summer over 5,000 people per day visit the top, so make sure to book ahead. Or come in June or September.

Tickets & reservations
We used a 5-day Interrail/Eurail Pass within one month, which proved especially convenient as it also covered journeys to and from Switzerland. Interrail/Eurail remains an excellent way to travel in countries where rail fares are generally high. Within Switzerland, the Swiss Travel Pass is another option, covering public transport and many museums. For the journey to Jungfraujoch, a separate ticket is required (details at jungfrau.ch) and this can be expensive, though occasional discounts are available. Holders of a Swiss Travel Pass or Interrail/Eurail Pass receive a 25% discount on the trip to the "Top of Europe," and no travel day is counted for this journey.

14 GERMANY - POLAND

BERLIN - ZAKOPANE

Poland, from the Baltic to the Tatras

We're standing on a ridge in the Tatra Mountains, one foot in Poland and one in Slovakia, when it occurs to us how far we've come. Five days ago, we boarded a train in Berlin. Since then, we've seen Baltic beaches, medieval fortresses, and a city rebuilt almost entirely from rubble. Now the peaks are turning gold in the last light, and we're not ready for the journey to end.

On a Thursday afternoon, we board the PKP Intercity service from Berlin Hauptbahnhof to Gdańsk Główny, a journey of just under six hours. The train is modern, with both open carriages and classic compartments, but the real highlight is the dining car – the *wagon restauracyjny* – identifiable by a bright red stripe along its exterior. Inside, the menu features Polish staples: pierogi stuffed with cheese or meat; a bowl of żurek, a sour rye soup; and szarlotka, a warm apple-and-cinnamon cake. We order it all, plus a few bottles of Łomża from one of Poland's last independent breweries. Central and Eastern Europe still know how to run a proper train dining car, and this one is no exception.

LEAVING GERMANY

Not long after passing through the forests of eastern Brandenburg, we reach Frankfurt an der Oder, the German border city split since 1945 from its Polish neighbour, Słubice. The River Oder marks 187 km (116 mi) of the modern border, and from the window we spot a post painted in German colours indicating the exact crossing point.

Moments later, we enter Wielkopolski, or Greater Poland, the region where the Polish state first took shape in the Middle Ages, and where castles, palaces and remnants of early industry still dot the landscape.

PASSING POZNAŃ

Between larger towns, the land opens out into long, flat stretches punctuated only by quiet stations with deserted platforms. Just as the solitude begins to feel a little melancholic, the train pulls into Poznań, a university city that once served as Poland's first capital. Its cathedral is the oldest in the country, and some of the earliest Polish kings were crowned here.

The city feels like a natural place to pause, and for a moment we consider hopping off. Poznań's colourful Old Market Square is only ten minutes from the station but in the end, we stay on board

and catch a final glimpse of the Town Hall, where two metal goats butt heads in the clock tower every day at noon.

GDAŃSK, A VIBRANT HANSEATIC CITY

When we finally arrive in Gdańsk, the dining car empties quickly. Gdańsk Główny, a grand neo-Renaissance station rebuilt after its wartime destruction, is only a fifteen-minute walk from the Golden Gate and the start of Ulica Długa, which leads straight into one of Europe's most beautifully restored old towns.

Once a major Hanseatic port, Gdańsk grew wealthy on trade, and that prosperity is still visible along Długa (Long Street) and Długi Targ (Long Market), where cafés and bars now occupy the ground floors of ornate merchant houses with elaborate façades. For a great view of the city and the river, the Sassy rooftop is hard to beat.

WHERE THE SECOND WORLD WAR BEGAN

Gdańsk's history is never far away. Just north of the centre lies the Westerplatte, the peninsula where the first shots of the Second World War were fired on 1st September 1939. We take a bus past abandoned shipyards to the tall granite monument that marks the site. Bunkers, ruins and a former Polish command post remain scattered across the peninsula. It's a quiet, sobering place where the scale of what followed is difficult to grasp. Back in the city, we visit the Museum of the Second World War, the largest war museum in Europe. The building itself is striking, angled into the ground like a piece of shrapnel, and the exhibitions inside are extensive.

THE SHIPYARD THAT CHANGED EUROPE

Gdańsk is also the birthplace of Solidarity, the workers' movement that helped bring down Poland's communist government. In 1980, led by the

charismatic Lech Wałęsa, thousands of shipyard workers walked out in protest, demanding basic rights and political reform. Their handwritten list of 21 demands is now UNESCO-listed and displayed at the European Solidarity Centre, a rust-coloured building overlooking the shipyards where the movement began.

After immersing ourselves in history, we take a short regional train to the Baltic coast for a change of scenery. Trains to Sopot run every ten minutes, and in just twelve minutes we step off at one of Poland's most elegant seaside towns. Its six-kilometre (3.5-mile) beach is glorious, and its wooden pier stretches 515 m (1,690 ft) into the sea, the longest of its kind in Europe. It's the perfect breather before the next stage of our journey.

MALBORK AND THE ROAD TO WARSAW

Fast Intercity trains link Gdańsk and Warsaw in about two and a half hours, and it's worth keeping an eye on the view. Shortly after leaving Tczew, the train crosses the Vistula, Poland's longest river and a cultural symbol so significant that the term *Kraj nad Wisłą* (Vistula Land) is sometimes used to refer to the country itself.

Within minutes, the enormous red-brick fortress of Malbork appears on the right. Built by the Teutonic Knights in the 13th century and expanded over nearly two hundred years, it contains around 4.5 million bricks and is the largest brick structure in the world. At its height, some 3,000 knights lived and worked within its walls. It's an extraordinary feat of medieval engineering and well worth a stop, only a fifteen-minute walk from either Malbork or Malbork Kałdowo stations.

A CITY REINVENTED

When we arrive at Warszawa Centralna, the skyline is dominated by the Palace of Culture and Science, Stalin's monumental postwar "gift" to Poland. Today it houses theatres, museums, a cinema and a viewing platform, and its ground floor is home to popular bars such as Kulturalna and Bar Studio, where we stop for a drink.

Warsaw's centre looks different from other Polish cities. Rather than growing around a single market square, it's an eclectic mix of restored medieval streets, Communist-era blocks and futuristic glass towers. Many of the main landmarks lie in Śródmieście, the central district surrounding the station, which is where we base ourselves for our stay.

SCARRED BUT RESILIENT

The scale of destruction in Warsaw during World War II is hard to comprehend. As we walk through the streets, we notice small markers in the pavement indicating the boundaries of the former Jewish Ghetto, the largest built by Nazi Germany, enclosed by a three-metre-high (10 ft) wall. A new Ghetto Museum is set to open soon in a former children's hospital, though debate already surrounds its political framing of the Holocaust. The Warsaw Rising Museum offers another perspective, telling the story of the 20,000 resistance fighters who took up arms against German occupation in 1944, in what became the largest resistance movement in occupied Europe.

THROUGH THE OLD TOWN

Despite its painful history, Warsaw today feels young and full of energy. From the Royal Castle we follow Krakowskie Przedmieście and Nowy Świat, two of the city's most elegant streets, before turning into the alleyways of the Old Town. Locals, however, prefer the Vistula riverfront, especially around Bulwary, where we sit by the water while a street musician plays Chopin in the evening light.

KRAKÓW AND THE FINAL STRETCH SOUTH

High-speed trains run from Warsaw to Kraków every hour. Poland's former royal capital is filled with cultural heritage and is one of the country's most visited cities. Since we've been before, we stay just one night and head straight to Kazimierz, the former Jewish quarter that's now packed with

excellent cafés, bars and restaurants. It's the perfect place to try fried oscypek cheese with berries, fruit-infused vodka, or any number of Polish comfort dishes.

INTO THE TATRAS

The final leg of our journey takes us to Zakopane, around 100 km (60 mi) south of Kraków. The train we choose is one of the most leisurely in the country, stopping 48 times as it winds through the countryside. The pace is meditative, unhurried. Gradually the landscape turns greener, and the mountains begin to rise ahead. The Tatra Mountains, a UNESCO Biosphere Reserve that form the natural border with Slovakia, are dramatic with sharp peaks, rocky cliffs and crystal-clear glacial lakes. With luck, you might even spot a brown bear, wolf or lynx.

After more than two and a half hours, our train arrives in Zakopane and everyone tumbles out. The town sits at the foot of Giewont mountain and is famous for its distinctive wooden villas, some of which have been turned into museums and guesthouses. One of the most impressive, Villa Koliba, houses the Zakopane Style Museum, which offers a glimpse into early twentieth-century mountain life.

GOLDEN PEAKS

Zakopane is both enchanting and a little overwhelming. Because Poland has only a small stretch of truly high mountains, everyone seems to gather here. Families with prams, day trippers, groups of hikers debating which trail to take all drift down Krupówki, Zakopane's lively main street, which is lined with wooden chalets and food stalls.

It's busy, but Zakopane has a secret. Take the cable car and the town quickly disappears beneath you, the noise fading away. Minutes later, you're surrounded by silence and open space. Push beyond the first viewpoint and the crowds thin out too, leaving just mountains and sky. We ride one of Europe's oldest cable cars up to Kasprowy Wierch, at 1,987 m (6,519 ft), where a short walk from the upper station brings us onto the border ridge between Poland and Slovakia.

It's day five of our trip, and we've reached the Tatras, where Poland ends and the valleys of Slovakia begin, and as the mountains turn gold in the last light, it feels like a fitting end to the journey, and one that leaves us wanting more.

JOURNEY DETAILS

Begins at Berlin Hauptbahnhof, Germany
Ends at Zakopane, Poland

Where you'll go
Berlin – Gdańsk, 6 hours
Gdańsk – Warsaw, 2.45 hours
Warsaw – Kraków, 2.45 hours
Kraków – Zakopane, 3 hours
From Zakopane, you can easily travel back to Kraków.

Time needed
At least 7 days; 10 days recommended for a relaxed pace. This is a wonderfully varied journey that combines Baltic beaches, major historic cities and some of Europe's most dramatic mountains, all connected by comfortable, frequent InterCity trains with surprisingly good on-board dining.

Tickets & reservations
An Interrail/Eurail Pass (7 days within 1 month) covers the whole route. Seat reservations are compulsory. Individual tickets in Poland may be cheaper if you book well in advance at intercity.pl.

15 GERMANY - AUSTRIA - ITALY

MUNICH - TRENTO

The Land of Lakes and Vineyards

There's something about boarding a southbound train in Munich. The Alps rise in the distance, hazy at first, growing sharper with every mile until they fill the window. Few journeys build anticipation quite like this one.

Five times a day, EuroCity and Railjet trains run from Munich over the Brenner Pass to Verona and onward to Venice, Bologna and Rimini. This time, though, we're leaving the big Italian cities behind. At Innsbruck we change onto a local train through South Tyrol and Trentino, ending in Trento – a smaller, quieter city that makes an ideal base for a few days of cycling between lakes, castles, and vineyards.

CASTLE COUNTRY

From Munich, the train heads east before sweeping south at Rosenheim, following the River Inn towards Tyrol. The first peaks above 1,000 m (3,280 ft) appear, and before long the mountains seem close enough to touch. Just across the Austrian border, the great fortress of Kufstein comes into view, located strategically on the border between Bavaria and Tyrol, fought over for centuries, and later used to imprison political dissidents during the Austro-Hungarian era. If you have time, hop off to visit the "Medieval Justice" exhibition in the old powder tower. It's an eye-opening look at how brutal the justice system once was.

FOLLOWING THE INN

Beyond Kufstein, the train hugs the river for nearly 80 km (50 mi), calling at towns like Wörgl and Brixlegg. At Jenbach, the bright red Zillertalbahn rattles 32 km (20 mi) into the famous Ziller Valley, crossing 35 bridges along the way, something we make a mental note to return for. Today, though, we press on to Innsbruck, the 800-year-old capital of Tyrol wedged between the Karwendel mountain range and the Tux Alps. We drop our bags in a locker and wander through the old town, past fifteenth- and sixteenth-century buildings to the famous Golden Roof, its 2,657 gilded tiles glinting in the afternoon light – a sight that has drawn visitors since 1500.

HUNGERBURGBAHN

From the Congress building, the Hungerburgbahn funicular climbs towards the Nordkette, one of Innsbruck's two local mountains. Designed by Zaha Hadid, the four stations look like sculpted shards of ice, startlingly futuristic against the traditional Tyrollean backdrop. We'll admit it: we're a little obsessed with trains. But there's something special about stations that manage to be both functional and beautiful.

At Hungerburg, a cable car carries us higher still. The Goetheweg trail traces the ridge, with the Karwendel massif on one side and the Inn Valley spread out far below. Goethe travelled through Tyrol on his Italian Journey and wrote often about the joy of walking in the mountains, although whether he ever trod this path is unknown.

OVER THE BRENNER

The next morning, we return to the tracks. Not on the direct EuroCity, which requires a ticket supplement, but on local trains that follow the same route at a gentler pace. The journey to Trento takes an hour longer and involves changing in Bolzano, but the slower rhythm suits us just fine.

South of Innsbruck, the train follows the River Sill through a narrowing valley. At St. Jodok am Brenner, we step onto the platform and find ourselves in a postcard: white church, red spire, green meadows, snow-capped mountains. Many stations on this stretch are built from local stone, solid and weathered, rooted in the landscape.

At Brenner, we cross into Italy, though it doesn't feel like it at first. South Tyrol is a province between worlds, Alpine and Mediterranean at the same time, home to vineyards, mountain farms and the pale peaks of the Dolomites. German, Italian and Ladin are all spoken here, and on

our train, even on the Italian side, every stop is announced first in German.

We follow the fast-flowing Isarco, and just after Vipiteno catch our first glimpse of Reifenstein Castle, one of South Tyrol's oldest and best preserved fortresses. The landscape remains wild, punctuated by more castles, all the way to Bolzano, the provincial capital that's been shaped by both Austrian and Italian cultures for centuries.

AN IMPREGNABLE FORTRESS

Shortly after the dark-timbered station at Fortezza and the reservoir beside it, an enormous stone structure fills the left-hand windows: Forte di Fortezza. Built in the 1830s at a cost equivalent to some €400 million today, it was such an extravagant undertaking that Emperor Franz I is said to have remarked that, for the amount he paid, he expected a fortress made out of silver. And yet despite its scale, it never saw battle. During the Second World War, the SS used it to store looted goods, and at one point Italy's national gold reserves were kept here as well. Today, it stands empty, save for a small museum.

CHURCHES ON EVERY HILLTOP

The two baroque towers of Bressanone Cathedral soon appear, followed by the church spires of Velturno. Most striking of all, however, is the Abbey of Sabiona, perched 200 m (656 ft) above Chiusa on a rocky hill, looking like something straight out of a fairytale. The last nuns left in 2021, but the buildings remain serene and imposing. Past Ora, the valley begins to open out. Orchards and vineyards, quiet villages and tiny stations nearly swallowed by vines. At Salorno, the final village before Trento, you could step off the train and walk straight into the vineyards. Bathed in late-afternoon light, the hills glow as we roll south.

A CITY BETWEEN TWO WORLDS

Trento's station, built of wood and reinforced concrete, replaced a more Austrian-looking building that Mussolini's regime demolished in the 1930s in an effort to "italianise" the region. From the

platform, it's only a short walk to Piazza Dante, where a statue of the poet stands at the centre and our hotel looks onto the square.

With around 120,000 residents, Trento feels compact and relaxed. Its history stretches back more than 2,000 years, traces of which survive at the Roman Villa di Orfeo, excavated beneath Via Rosmini. A short walk from the station also brings you to the thirteenth-century Castello del Buonconsiglio, the largest of the city's five castles, as well as the cathedral and Torre Civica tower.

On Piazza Duomo, beside the Neptune fountain, we settle at a table at Caffè Italia, mountains rising behind us and espresso close at hand. Yet, like nearby Bolzano, Trento sits between cultures. Beer is ordered as readily as wine, polenta and speck appear alongside pasta and olive oil. It feels neither fully Austrian nor entirely Italian, but something in between. Perhaps that's why the city has such a distinct character: few tourists, no souvenir shops, just locals sitting in cafés and getting on with their day.

Later, we take the Funivia Trento–Sardagna, a cable car that climbs 600 m (1,970 ft) in four minutes. From the Busa degli Orsi viewpoint, we look out over Trento, the Adige glinting below, snowy peaks on the horizon. Far down in the valley, trains inch along like toys. When we return to the riverbank, the heat has intensified, and we cool off with an ice-cold granita at Bar Funivia.

A BRANCH LINE TOWARDS VENICE

The following day, we take the local train to Levico Terme, planning to cycle between some of the region's many lakes and castles. Soon after leaving Trento, the train begins a steep climb, the city receding behind us. It follows the River Brenta to its high point at Pergine Valsugana (468 m, or 1,535 ft), then drops past Lake Caldonazzo before arriving in Levico. Trentino has nearly 300 lakes, though on this trip we see only a handful.

From Levico, the single-track Valsugana line continues east through the valley towards Bassano del Grappa, where it connects with trains to Venice.

It's a quieter alternative to the main Brenner–Venice route. Less travelled, but full of small surprises. Originally a private Austrian railway, it once carried Empress Elisabeth "Sisi" of Austria, who often stayed at the imperial summer residence in Levico. Watching the landscape unfold, it's easy to understand why she loved this route.

ECHOES OF VENICE

We hire bikes and follow the River Brenta eastward from Levico to Borgo Valsugana along quiet cycle paths, passing meadows, orchards and the occasional farmhouse. High above the valley, Castel Telvana keeps watch. After 15 km (9 mi), we reach Borgo Valsugana, an old town with a distinctly Venetian character: riverfront houses, stone gates, faded frescoes and small architectural flourishes that reflect centuries of influence.

On the way back, we stop for a swim in Lake Levico, which has been awarded a European Blue Flag for its pristine waters, and as evening settles, climb to Castel Pergine for an aperitivo and to take in the view over the blue expanse of Lake Caldonazzo. It's quiet but beatiful end to our journey before the train carries us north again.

JOURNEY DETAILS

Begins at Munich Hauptbahnhof, Germany
Ends at Trento, Italy

Munich is easily reached by direct trains from Amsterdam, Zurich, Vienna and Berlin. From Trento, you can travel on to Verona and Venice.

Where you'll go
Munich – Innsbruck, 2 hours
Innsbruck – Trento, change in Bolzano, 2.5 hours
Trento – Levico Terme, 45 min

Time needed
This trip can be done in a long weekend. One week is ideal. While most travellers continue to Verona or Venice, we stopped in Trento, capital of Trentino, and explored the single-track branch line through the Valsugana Valley.

Tickets & reservations
We used a 4-day Interrail/Eurail Pass (valid for one month).

16 FRANCE - SPAIN

PARIS - ZARAGOZA

The Pyrenees' Forgotten Station

In 1928, at the height of Europe's railway age, you could board a train in Paris and travel all the way to Madrid, crossing the Pyrenees through a tunnel blasted into the mountains. The line ran from Pau in France to Canfranc in Spain, one of the great engineering achievements of its age. The route closed long ago, but you can still follow most of the journey today, first by train to the French village of Bedous and then by bus over the border to Canfranc, where one of Europe's most extraordinary stations stands waiting in the mountains. After a quick visit, we hop on the train to Zaragoza.

PARIS TO BORDEAUX

The journey begins at Paris Montparnasse, where the TGV to Bordeaux leaves several times a day. The train covers 500 km (300 mi) in just two hours, racing through flat farmland at up to 320 km/h (200 mph). The scenery is pleasant rather than dramatic, with green fields and small villages sliding by, but there's something hypnotic about watching France unfold from the window. "Laissez-vous rêver," say the stickers on the windows. Let yourself dream. And then, almost before you notice, Bordeaux appears.

Bordeaux-Saint-Jean is worth a few minutes of your time. The station's iron and glass canopy, built in 1898, is the largest in Europe, constructed by the same firm that made the Grand Palais in Paris. Inside the entrance hall, a 1929 mural depicts the French rail network of the time. Memorials in the station remember darker chapters of history too, such as the Train Fantôme, a deportation train that carried nearly 700 people through France in the summer of 1944.

Another commemorates Charles Domercq, the stationmaster who helped organise escape routes to Spain during the Nazi occupation.

THROUGH THE LANDES FOREST

From Bordeaux, we change to a regional train heading south through one of the emptiest parts of France. The Forêt des Landes de Gascogne covers 13,000 km² (5,000 sq mi) and was planted in the eighteenth and nineteenth centuries to drain the marshes and stabilise the sandy soil. Before the forest, this was swampland where only a few shepherds eked out a living. Attempts to cultivate rice, peanuts, and tobacco all failed until Napoleon III ordered the land planted in 1857, and today the forest stretches in all directions. The train passes through quietly, stopping at villages that feel far from anywhere. At Labouheyre, eighty plane trees planted by Napoleon III shade the main square, and a Sunday market sells local produce. At Morcenx, the track straightens into a line so perfect that, in the 1950s, it was used to set the world rail speed record of 331 km/h (206 mph). Then at Dax, the line divides, with one branch heading west towards the Atlantic coast and the Spanish border at Hendaye, while we continue south towards Pau and the Pyrenees.

PAU

Pau sits at the foot of the mountains, looking up at a line of peaks that stretches along the horizon. Until the First World War, it was a fashionable resort, especially popular with the English, who came for the clean mountain air and even established continental Europe's first golf course here. The station, down in the lower town, opened in 1863. A funicular still carries passengers up the steep hill to the Boulevard des Pyrénées, where the view on a clear day reaches all the way to the Pic du Midi d'Ossau, an ancient volcano rising to 2,884 m (9,462 ft) near the Spanish border.

INTO THE MOUNTAINS

The railcar growls and lurches forward before slowly pulling away from the platform. Within minutes, Pau has disappeared and we're in open

country, crossing the River Ousse and climbing into the foothills of the Pyrenees. Branches scrape against the windows. The stations we pass through have seen better days, some boarded up, others converted into houses. On the old stone walls, faded paint still shows the original departmental name, Basses-Pyrénées, alongside the altitude in metres.

At Oloron-Sainte-Marie, most passengers get off. The town has a cathedral on the UNESCO World Heritage list, part of the pilgrimage route to Santiago de Compostela, and medieval streets worth exploring, but we stay on the train, now nearly empty, as it follows the Gave d'Aspe river deeper into the valley. The mountains rise on either side, green and steep. The driver leaves his cab door open, and we watch over his shoulder as the track curves ahead.

Bedous, when we arrive, is a small village with a lovingly restored station that now operates as an eleven-room hotel, a red signal marking the end of the line.

THE ROAD TO CANFRANC

The tracks from Bedous to Canfranc have been closed since 1970, when a derailment on the French side gave authorities an excuse to abandon a line that was already losing money. Thirty kilometres (18.5 mi) of railway now lie silent in the mountains, though there are plans, endlessly discussed, to restore the connection.

For now, buses make the journey, following the old route through the Vallée d'Aspe. Along the way, you see what remains of the railway: viaducts spanning gorges, tunnel mouths dark against the rock, station buildings crumbling at Lescun and Urdos. The old station at Etsaut has become an information centre for the Pyrenees National Park. Above it, cut into the cliff, stands the Fort du Portalet, where the Vichy regime imprisoned resistance fighters and where Marshal Pétain was held briefly after the war. The bus climbs higher, crossing into Spain through the Somport Tunnel, and then descends into the valley on the other side. And there, appearing suddenly below, is Canfranc.

THE STATION AT THE END OF THE WORLD

The station at Canfranc is enormous, a 241-metre (790 ft) palace of stone and glass with 150 doors and more than 350 windows, rising in a village of barely 600 people. It looks like something that belongs in Paris or Vienna, not in a remote valley in the Pyrenees. When it opened in 1928, newspapers compared it to the Titanic. They called it La Grande Dame des Pyrénées.

The station made sense in the context of its time. The Pau–Canfranc line was one of four crossings between France and Spain, built when railways were symbols of national prestige and international cooperation. The engineering was extraordinary. Rivers were diverted, viaducts thrown across valleys, tunnels bored through solid rock. The Tunnel de Sayerce, where trains spiralled inside the mountain to gain 60 m (200 ft) of altitude, was considered a masterpiece.

RESTORED GRANDEUR

Then came the war. As German bombs destroyed the other Franco-Spanish rail links, Canfranc became the only functioning crossing, and the only place in Spain ever occupied by Nazi forces. In 1942, swastika flags flew above the platforms. What happened next remains one of the darker episodes of the war. Hitler needed tungsten for his weapons industry and Franco wanted gold. At Canfranc, freight trains arrived from Germany loaded with plundered treasure and left carrying Spanish ore. Some historians believe this secret trade, conducted at a remote mountain station, may have prolonged the war by as much as two years.

After the line closed in 1970, the station fell into decay. For decades, it stood empty, its windows broken, its halls slowly filling with dust. Then, in

January 2023, it reopened as a five-star hotel, the grandeur restored and the history preserved, and today, Canfranc is a destination in its own right.

DESERTED LANDSCAPE

From Canfranc, a slow regional train runs twice daily to Zaragoza, serving fifteen minor intermediate stations and crossing one of the most sparsely populated regions of Spain. The northeast of the country, around the towns of Jaca, Huesca and Zaragoza, has an average population density of just eight inhabitants per square kilometre and is often referred to as Spain's demographic desert. Travelling by train through this landscape, occasional small villages or solitary churches appear, but for long stretches there is little more than open land, silence, and sky.

JOURNEY DETAILS

Begins at Paris Montparnasse, France
Ends at Zaragoza Delicias, Spain

Where you'll go
Paris – Bordeaux, 2 hours
Bordeaux – Pau, 2.5 hours
Pau – Bedous, 1.5 hours
Bedous – Canfranc, bus, 1 hour
Canfranc – Zaragoza, 3.5 hours

Zaragoza is well connected by fast trains to Barcelona and Madrid.

Time needed
One week is ideal, but we recommend staying much longer, exploring Bordeaux, hiking in the Pyrenees, taking a side trip to Arcachon, and discovering the less touristy regions of Les Landes and Aragon.

Tickets & reservations
Interrail/Eurail Passes cover all trains. Reservations are required for the TGV from Paris to Bordeaux. The bus from Bedous to Canfranc (5 departures daily) requires a separate ticket.

17 FRANCE — SPAIN — MOROCCO

PARIS - MARRAKECH

From the Seine to the Sahara

The promise of the desert pulls us south as our TGV tears through France at 300 km/h (186 mph). Two days and over 2,000 km (1,240 mi) later, we're at Europe's edge: the beach at Tarifa, in southern Spain. Surfers battle the waves where the Mediterranean meets the Atlantic, the sun sinking into the sea behind them. Across the Strait of Gibraltar, barely visible at dusk, lies Morocco. A few lights flicker on along the coast where tomorrow we'll arrive by ferry and continue south by rail.

THROUGH ANDALUSIA

The route from Paris to the tip of Spain is relatively straightforward, taking the TGV through France, then Spain's high-speed AVE via Barcelona and Madrid. But south of Madrid, we deliberately slow down. The landscape becomes more varied, with wooded hills, cotton fields, and the occasional fortress, the most striking of which is Castillo de Almodóvar del Río, an Arab-built hilltop citadel from the 8th century so picturesque it was used as a filming location for Game of Thrones.

At Antequera-Santa Ana we trade the slick AVE for a slower local Renfe train for the final stretch to Algeciras. The route through the Serranía de Ronda is worth savouring, with its whitewashed villages on distant hillsides, hemmed in by a dramatic wall of mountains. Despite the southern latitude, this is one of the rainiest pockets of Andalusia, and the valley we pass through is surprisingly lush.

Most stations along the line are charming, with sherbet-coloured buildings and orange trees growing on the platforms. By the time you reach Ronda, with its Moorish baths, Roman theatres and palaces, North Africa already feels close.

VALLEYS AND CAVES

Beyond Ronda, the train follows the River Guadiaro through narrowing valleys and gorges. Limestone cliffs rise on both sides, forest pressing close, rivers flashing past. Centuries of heavy rain have carved spectacular ravines across the Sierra de Grazalema – including the Garganta Verde, which drops 400 m (1,310 ft) – and created vast underground systems like Hundidero-Gato. One cave here runs for 10 km (6 mi) and is home to one of Spain's largest bat colonies.

THE EDGE OF EUROPE

Soon, as we approach the coast and the southernmost station in Europe, the Rock of Gibraltar appears on the horizon. Algeciras is a working port that feels a little rough around the edges, but it's only a short walk to the maritime terminal where you can catch a bus to Tarifa. We could board the ferry to Tangier immediately, but Tarifa deserves at least a brief stop, with its long beaches, whitewashed old town and excellent tapas bars. Above the town stands the castle of Alonso Pérez de Guzmán, known as Guzmán el Bueno. In the late 13th century, when Moors besieged the city and captured his son, threatening to kill the boy unless he surrendered, Guzmán refused. Legend says he threw down his own dagger to the attackers, telling them to do their worst. Tragically, they did.

CROSSING TO AFRICA

At its narrowest point, the Strait of Gibraltar is only 14 km (9 mi) wide, and for years engineers have discussed building a tunnel between the two sides. The distance is significantly shorter than that between Dover and Calais, but the fault lines where the Eurasian and African tectonic plates meet make construction far more complex.

For now, the ferry from Tarifa remains the fastest option, arriving at Tangier's old port right beside the medina. The crossing takes less than an hour, and we watch the old town rising above the harbour as we approach. When we disembark, a long line of women in brightly coloured veils moves slowly through the terminal. Immediately, it's clear we've entered a different world.

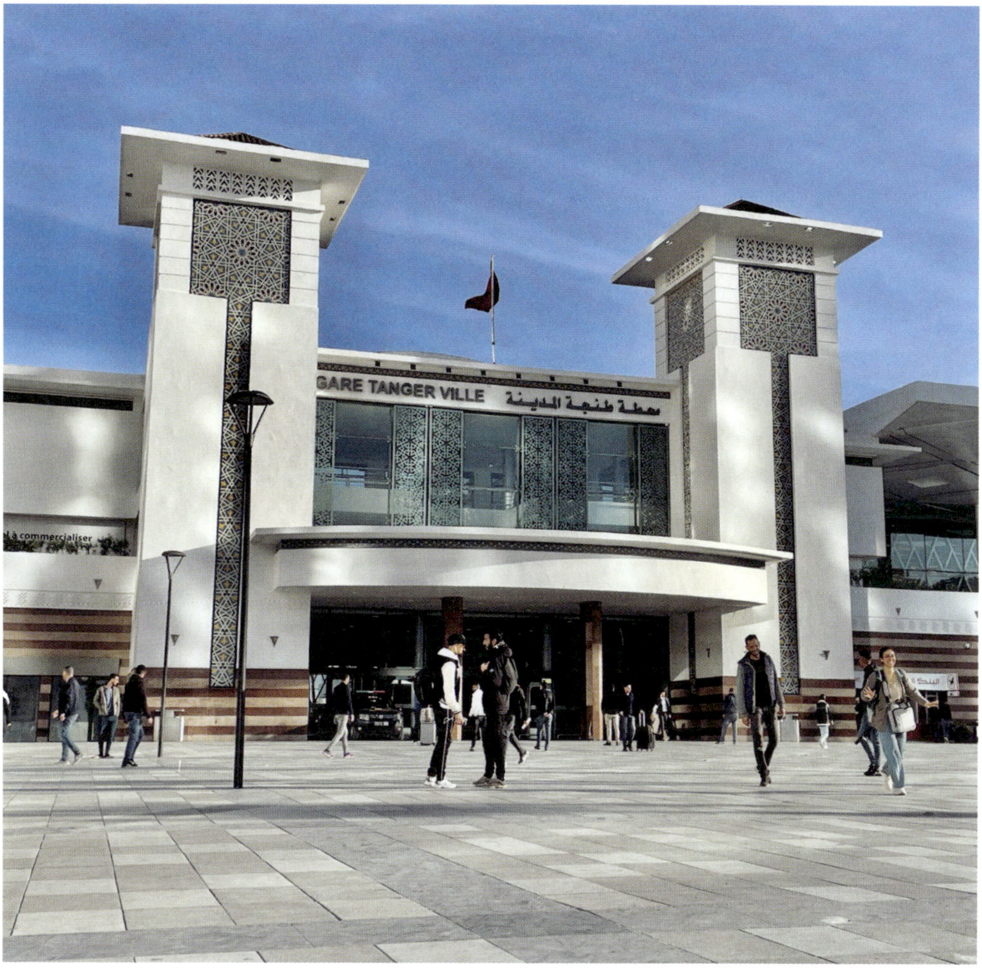
GARE TANGER VILLE
محطة طنجة المدينة

البحر الأبيض المتوسط
Mer Méditerranée
المحيط الأطلسي
Océan Atlantique

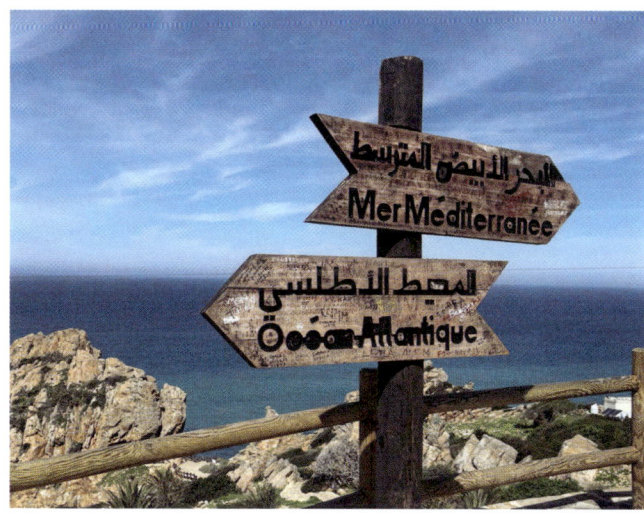

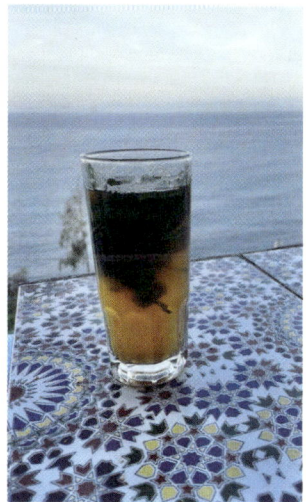

BACK IN TIME IN TANGIER

We spend our first night at the Hôtel Continental, a 19th-century landmark built on the site of the old customs house. The guestbook is filled with the names of artists, aristocrats and adventurers, including Winston Churchill, who stayed here after his time as a war correspondent. Gaudí supposedly slept here too, while planning a cathedral for Tangier that was never built. With a mix of English furnishings and Moorish details, and a terrace that overlooks the bay, the hotel feels like a place where the two continents meet.

SPIES AND SMUGGLERS

Few traces remain of Tangier's time as an International Zone (1923-1956), when France, Spain and Britain jointly administered the city and it became a magnet for spies, smugglers, writers and exiles. During the Second World War, Tangier played a strategic role as the Allies prepared Operation Torch. Agents moved through the alleys, meeting in cafés, disappearing into the medina. The era inspired countless novels and films, including *The Bourne Ultimatum*, which shot several scenes in these streets.

Some of the city's cafés take you back to that time. The Grand Café de Paris has kept its 1940s feel, for instance. Then there's Gran Café Central on Place Petit Socco, which is perfect for watching street performers and locals meeting over mint tea. Down by the cliffs, Café Hafa, largely unchanged since 1921, offers views across the strait. Groups of young men play board games on the terrace, and the scent of hash occasionally drifts past.

After exploring the old town, we take a taxi to Cape Spartel, the northwestern tip of Africa. A lighthouse here overlooks the point where the Mediterranean and Atlantic meet, the coastline stretching for miles in both directions. Below, the wide golden beach at Achakkar curves away to the south, the water glistening a deep blue.

AFRICA'S FASTEST TRAIN

Next morning, we take a *petit taxi* to Tanger-Ville station for the Al Boraq, Africa's first high-speed train. Since 2018, it's connected Tangier with Casablanca in just over two hours, covering 323 km (200 mi) at speeds up to 320 km/h (200 mph). The train feels like a French TGV – comfortable, quiet, punctual – and we leave exactly on time, the Atlantic appearing briefly beside us before the line turns inland.

AL ATLAS

We travel as far as Kénitra, about an hour south, where we change to the traditional Al Atlas service. The contrast is immediate. The orange-and-white paintwork is peeling, the carriages creak and rattle. Some doors stay open even as the train reaches 100 km/h (62 mph), passengers leaning out into the wind, fresh air pouring in.

The route from Kénitra to Fès is beautiful, moving gradually from coast into rolling countryside. Stations are announced in Arabic and French, and each has its own character. Sidi Yahya, with red flowers and orange trees along the platform, could almost be in southern Spain. Much of the journey runs through farmland – donkeys carrying loads, shepherds tending flocks, teenagers playing football beside the tracks – and the stretch of railway just before Meknès is one of the highlights of the entire route.

THE MEDINA OF FÈS

Set in a valley of orchards and olive groves, Fès is one of Morocco's most beautiful historic cities. Often described as the "Mecca of the West", Fès has also long been seen as Morocco's spiritual and intellectual centre. The Medina – a UNESCO World Heritage site and reportedly the world's largest pedestrian zone – is a maze of 9,000 alleys, 70,000 residents, and thousands of shops and workshops.

We spend hours walking, getting lost, cooling off on rooftop terraces like the one at Fondouk Bazaar. That night we stay in a riad, a traditional house built around a cool, central courtyard, and wake to a donkey braying somewhere close by. At times the noise and the intensity of the medina can feel overwhelming, so we walk up to the Marinid Tombs for some space, the hillside around us dotted with olive trees and wild lavender. The city stretches out below: minarets, rooftops, tanneries. Mount Zalagh, rising even higher above the city, offers wider views across the valley, but we're content to stay here.

SOUTH TO MARRAKECH

After a short stay in Fès – one night barely scratches the surface, two or three full days would be better – we board the direct train to Marrakech. Several services run daily via Kénitra and Casablanca, so we retrace our route toward the coast before continuing another four hours south. For a brief stretch, the line runs parallel to the

shore, though we never quite see the sea. Instead, there are glimpses of everyday life. Houses at Gare de Salé-Tabriquet with front gardens spilling onto the platform, laundry drying on balconies, children playing between the tracks.

By the time we reach Casablanca, dusk has fallen. It's tempting to stop – there's plenty to see in the "White City" – but with three hours still to go, we continue our journey. Outside, the last daylight turns the landscape a deep orange-brown, and when we finally do roll into Marrakech, we open Spotify and put on "Marrakesh Express" by Crosby, Stills & Nash. The perfect arrival soundtrack.

THE RED CITY

Trains first reached Marrakech in 1923. The original sand-coloured station still stands beside the tracks, but in 2008 it was replaced by a striking new terminal, a palatial glass building that incorporates traditional Moroccan patterns, vast and bright. Marrakech was founded nearly a thousand years ago by the Berbers, built in the warm terracotta colours of the Haouz plain that give it the name "the Red City." Its 19-kilometre (12-mile) wall, constructed in the 11th century, remains almost intact. At the centre lies Jemaa el-Fnaa, the beating heart of the city-some say of the whole country. Each evening, the square transforms: snake charmers, storytellers, musicians, crowds gathering around performers. Fruit juice stands appear, food stalls fire up their grills for *méchoui* – slow-roasted lamb, a national favourite – while the surrounding souks spread out in a maze of narrow lanes where you can wander for hours.

We finish our journey on a medina rooftop, watching the city lights come on as the Atlas Mountains fade into darkness. After two days of heat, noise and crowds, we're ready for a change and the next morning we head to Imlil, a pretty Berber village at 1,800 m (5,900 ft). As the gateway to Mount Toubkal, Morocco's highest peak and the tallest in North Africa, it offers cool air, mountain views and quiet. Exactly what we need before we venture into the desert.

JOURNEY DETAILS

Begins in Paris Gare de Lyon, France
Ends at Marrakech, Morocco

Where you'll go
Paris – Madrid, 10 hours
Madrid – Ronda, change at Antequera-Santa Ana, 4 hours
Ronda – Algeciras, 2 hours
Algeciras – Tarifa, bus, 30 min
Tarifa – Tangier, ferry, 1 hour
Tangier – Fès, 4.5 hours (or Al Boraq with 1 change in Kénitra)
Fès – Marrakech, 6.5 hours

Time needed
In theory, Paris to Marrakech can be done in three days and two nights. But there's simply too much to see along the way, with an almost endless choice of rewarding stop-overs. Once in Morocco, it's well worth making side trips to the coast, such as Essaouira, as well as to the Sahara or the Atlas Mountains. Two weeks should be considered the absolute minimum for this journey.

Tickets & reservations
We used an Interrail/Eurail Pass for the journey to Europe's southernmost station. Until 2006, Interrail was also valid in Morocco, but the country has since withdrawn from the scheme. Rail travel within Morocco remains straightforward: tickets are easy to purchase via the Moroccan national railway website (ONCF) and are generally inexpensive. Ferries run from Tarifa directly to the old town of Tangier.

EPIC LONG-DISTANCE JOURNEYS

With the exception of a few routes, all routes on the following pages are included in the Interrail/Eurail Pass.

1
Hungaria
Hamburg - Budapest (13 hours)

One train, four countries, three rivers. The Hungaria follows the banks of the Elbe, the Vltava and the Danube, linking a string of real gems along the way: Hamburg, Berlin, Dresden, Prague, Bratislava and Budapest. It's one of Europe's oldest and longest direct international connections, over 1,200 km (745 mi) in length. It's an unforgettable journey packed with cultural highlights, stunning scenery and, conveniently, a reliably cold beer on board.

The original route ran from Berlin via Dresden, Prague, Brno and Bratislava to Budapest, but since 2015 the train has started in Hamburg. The first direct rail services between Berlin and Budapest appeared at the end of the 19th century, departing from the iconic Anhalter Bahnhof. During the Cold War, politicians and spies were frequent passengers, as were East German families allowed to holiday in Hungary.

Today the train is a comfortable Railjet, and you can still travel daily from Hamburg to Budapest in under 13 hours.

2
Bergensbanen
Oslo - Bergen (7 hours)

The Bergensbanen is widely considered one of the world's great railway journeys. Seven hours, 182 tunnels, more than 300 bridges, and scenery that shifts constantly as you travel from the gentle lowlands around Oslo into the heart of Norway. Valleys give way to high plateaux, then mountains, and finally the deep blue of the fjords. Much of the route is inaccessible by road.

Building the line was extraordinarily hard work. Around 2,400 workers spent fifteen years on it, carving tunnels from solid rock by hand in bitter cold. When King Haakon VII opened the railway in 1909, he called it a feat of daring. That still feels like the right description.

For the first hundred kilometres (62 miles) or so out of Oslo, the train keeps up a reasonable pace. Then the landscape closes in, the speed drops, and you're grateful for the extra time to take it all in.

Bergensbanen

Montenegro Express

3 Montenegro Express
Belgrade - Bar (11 hours)

This railway was one of Tito's most ambitious projects. As leader of communist Yugoslavia, he was determined to link Belgrade with the Adriatic coast, even though the Dinaric Alps lay directly in between. The result is one of Europe's most dramatic rail journeys: 520 km (323 mi) of track crossing 435 bridges and passing through 254 tunnels. The standout moment is the Mala Rijeka Viaduct, which soars 200 m 656 ft) above a gorge, making it the highest railway bridge in Europe.

Tito himself was a keen traveller by train. He owned a private blue carriage and used it to tour Yugoslavia, with an extraordinary list of guests over the years, including Queen Elizabeth II, Charles de Gaulle, François Mitterrand, Yasser Arafat, Sophia Loren and Elizabeth Taylor.

Two trains run each day. The most impressive section is between Mojkovac and Bar, so it's worth planning your journey to travel this stretch in daylight. If eleven hours on one train feels like too much, you can still experience the best scenery by taking local services from Podgorica, Montenegro's capital.

4 Transalpin
Graz - Zurich (9.5 hours)

The longest direct journey through the Alps is the EuroCity Transalpin, which runs daily from Graz in Austria (2.5 hours south of Vienna) to Zurich in Switzerland. It's a true Alpine crossing with spectacular views throughout.

Shortly after leaving Graz, the train climbs over the Schober Pass at 849 m (2,785 ft). Past Bischofshofen, you enter the Salzach Valley, where the railway weaves along the river through tunnels and over bridges. The route continues past Zell am See, where the crystal-clear lake mirrors the surrounding peaks. You might catch a glimpse of the Kitzsteinhorn at 3,203 m (10,509 ft) near Kaprun and its year-round snow before the train passes well-known ski resorts like Kitzbühel on its way through Tyrol to Innsbruck.

From there, the line climbs toward St. Anton am Arlberg, which at 1,304 m (4,278 ft) is the highest station on the route. A highlight is the Trisanna Bridge, an engineering marvel built in 1884 that stands 87 m (285 ft) above the valley floor. Between Feldkirch and Buchs you briefly pass through Liechtenstein and cross the Rhine, which forms the border with Switzerland. Soon you're skirting the emerald-green waters of Lake Walen. As you approach Zurich, the mountains recede, but the views over Lake Zurich are just as inviting. It's a magnificent journey from start to finish, complete with a dining car and first-class panoramic coaches.

Walensee

5   Torre del Oro
Barcelona - Cádiz (13 hours)

For more than seventy years, a direct train has run from Barcelona-Sants to Seville, and in recent years it has continued all the way to Cádiz on the Atlantic coast. The Torre del Oro – named after Seville's 13th-century golden watchtower – cuts across some of Spain's most beautiful and sparsely populated landscapes.

The journey begins among rolling hills of olive groves and vineyards, with flashes of the Mediterranean in the distance. After Valencia, the train crosses three hours of sun-baked plateau before entering Andalusia through the dramatic Despeñaperros gorge, the only natural passage through the 400-km (200-mi) Sierra Morena. From there, whitewashed hill towns appear one after another. It's one of Spain's great inland rail journeys.

MOUNTAIN ADVENTURES

6   Semmering Railway
Vienna - Semmering (1 hour, 15 mins)

Vienna is the starting point for the world's first mountain railway, and the line remains a pleasure to travel today. Semmering is less than ninety minutes away, and once a day a train continues from there all the way to Trieste on the Adriatic.

The Semmering Railway was built between 1848 and 1854, covering 41 km (25 mi) of mountain terrain. Around 10,000 workers constructed 14 tunnels and 16 viaducts, climbing 450 m (1,476 ft) in altitude. This was before the age of mechanical drills, so every tunnel had to be cut by hand. It was an astonishing achievement.

The quality of the construction was such that the line never closed. It runs through beautiful mountain scenery, and in the railway's early years the Semmering Pass became a fashionable retreat for Viennese high society. You can still see the grand villas and hotels they built along the route.

7   Bernina Express
Chur - Tirano (4 hours, 20 mins)

There's a reason the red Bernina Express is one of Switzerland's best-known trains. Over the course of four hours, it climbs steadily through some of the country's most impressive scenery, passing glaciers, rushing mountain streams and peaks rising above 4,000 m (13,000 ft). Along the way, it crosses dozens of bridges and viaducts before finally reaching the Bernina Pass at 2,253 m (7,392 ft). The stretch between Thusis and Poschiavo is a UNESCO World Heritage Site, though honestly the whole journey is spectacular.

The moment everyone waits for is the Landwasser Viaduct near Filisur. The train emerges from a tunnel, curves across a stone bridge high above a forested gorge, and vanishes into another tunnel on the far side. Built in 1901 and 1902 without scaffolding and using only two cranes, it's as impressive from an engineering point of view as it is from the window. The large panoramic windows make the most of the view, and in summer open-air carriages make taking photos even easier.

Before the railway was built, this journey took around fourteen hours by mail coach. The train reduced it to just two. Around 5,000 workers completed the line in only five years, which you can learn more about at the Albula Railway Museum, right next to Bergün station. You don't have to take the Express. Regional trains from Rhätische Bahn run along the same route. It's excellent walking country, and the Via Albula-Bernina trail allows you to hike between stations at your own pace.

Landwasser Viaduct, Bernina & Glacier Express

8 Glacier Express
St. Moritz or Davos - Zermatt (7.5 hours)

Yes, this is the famous tourist train, and reservations are required. But if you'd rather be more flexible, regional trains cover the same route without needing to book ahead.
 It takes slightly longer and involves 4 transfers, but the views are identical. You crawl across 291 bridges, through 91 tunnels, and over gradients made possible only by cogwheel technology. Terrain steep enough to make a mountain goat jealous. From deep gorges (including the Rhine Gorge) to ancient forests and Alpine meadows, the landscapes shift constantly before culminating in the shadow of the Matterhorn. The literal high point is the Oberalp Pass at 2,033 m (6,670 ft).

Glacier Express route

MOUTAIN ADVENTURES

Lake Geneva

9   **EuroCity Geneva - Milan**
*Geneva - Cornavin - Milano Centrale
(4 hours)*

Running four times a day, this regular Intercity service is one of Europe's most beautiful train journeys. Just after leaving Geneva, the line follows the vineyard-covered shores of the city's lake. After Lausanne, you're treated to sweeping views of terraced vines, glittering water and the peaks of France's Haute-Savoie and Switzerland's Valais.

An hour of mountains and lakes later, the train enters the Rhône Valley, flanked by three- and four-thousand-metre summits and yet more vineyards around Sion. Emerging from the tunnel after Brig, you wind through the Italian Alps along the western shore of Lake Maggiore towards Milan. The final stretch is calmer after all the Alpine drama, but arriving at Milano Centrale, one of Europe's largest and most opulent stations, will jolt you awake.

At Montreux, you can also change onto the Golden-Pass Express to Interlaken via Zweisinnen. (See our chapter 'Above the Clouds at Jungfraujoch', page 179.)

10   **Through the Ardennes**
Liège - Luxembourg City (2.5 hours)

This journey begins with a station worth arriving early for. Liège-Guillemins, designed by Santiago Calatrava, is a sweeping canopy of steel and glass, and trains glide in and out beneath it almost silently. Even if you've seen photographs, the building is striking in person.

From Liège, the InterCity heads south into the Ardennes, calling at small stations along the way. Coo has its famous waterfalls. Vielsalm has a lake. Clervaux sits in a valley beneath a castle. Any of them would reward a longer stop.

Luxembourg City, at the end of the line, is worth the trip in its own right. It's compact, handsome and easy to get around. Public transport throughout the country is free, including second-class trains, so you can explore without spending a penny on fares.

11 Brenner Route
Munich - Verona (5.5 hours)

Another Alpine crossing, this time from north to south, which takes you from the Bavarian Alps through Tyrol into Italy's Trentino region through some spectacular scenery. (See our chapter 'The Land of Lakes and Vineyards', page 197).

12 Mont-Blanc Express
Martigny - Saint-Gervais-les-Bains (2.5 hours)

The red-and-white carriages of the Mont-Blanc Express may lack the glamour of the Glacier or Bernina Express, but for more than a century they've linked the Swiss Rhône Valley with the French villages at the foot of Mont Blanc, including Chamonix.

From Martigny, the train follows the River Trient through forests and tiny hamlets. Travelling at just 45 km/h (28 mph), you have time to spot chamois darting up the slopes.

The line required 21 tunnels, 16 avalanche shelters, 6 bridges and 5 viaducts, and many of its stops are request-only. It remains the quickest way through the Trient Valley, where the old postal road is still closed to cars. If you continue to the terminus at Saint-Gervais-les-Bains, you can connect with the Tramway du Mont-Blanc to Le Nid d'Aigle at 2,370 m (7,776 ft), the highest railway station in France.

Mont-Blanc Express

ISLAND RAILWAYS

13 Crossing the Wadden Sea
Hamburg - Westerland (Sylt)
(3 hours)

Not many trains run through the sea, but here in northern Germany, an 8-kilometre (5-mile) causeway carries a railway line across the Wadden Sea to Westerland on the island of Sylt.

Heading north from Hamburg, you watch the land flatten and the station names become more Nordic: Itzehoe, Husum, Niebüll, Klanxbüll. After Niebüll the train creeps along a single track through empty marshland, and then just beyond Klanxbüll it reaches the Hindenburg Dam. For the next few minutes, there's water on both sides.

Sylt is excellent for walking and cycling. From Westerland it's about 20 km (12 mi) by bike to Germany's northernmost point, just 4 km (2.5 mi) from Denmark. Half the island is a nature reserve, with sandy beaches, rolling dunes, heathland and sea cliffs.

14 Sicily, Mallorca, Corsica and Sardinia
There are more than 4,000 islands in the Mediterranean, but only four have railways.

Sicily has by far the largest network, with over 1,300 km (800 mi) of track. You can reach the island from the Italian mainland by train ferry, with the entire train rolling onto the boat at Villa San Giovanni. It's quite something to experience. (See page 129.)

Mallorca has oranges to thank for its railway. In the early 1900s, a fast connection was needed between Palma and the fruit-growing interior, so in 1912 the Ferrocarril de Sóller opened. It's the oldest line on the island, and the hour-long journey to the mountain village of Sóller takes you through almond, olive and citrus groves, over viaducts and through tunnels. Sóller itself is a handsome old town with narrow streets and an impressive church.

Corsica has what you might call a beach train. Several times a day it runs between Calvi and Île-Rousse, covering 22 km (14 mi) in 50 minutes with 18 stops along the way. On one side is the sea, on the other the mountains, and every station tempts you to get off. Some of the trains are modern, but others are 1970s carriages that rattle and sway and sound their horns before every bend. The windows open, so you can lean out if you like. It's a lovely reminder of how train travel used to feel.

Sardinia is home to the Trenino Verde, a narrow-gauge network that winds 438 km (272 mi) through the island's wild interior. It's the longest tourist railway in Europe, and the routes are wonderfully indirect. The story goes that the companies laying the track were paid by the kilometre, which would explain all the curves. At an average speed of 20 km/h (12 mph), there's plenty of time to watch the forests, lakes and hilltop villages roll past. The trains are vintage, the stations even more so. Nobody is in a hurry here, but that's rather the point.

Corsica

Mallorca

Rügen

15 Baltic islands

Germany has more than fifty Baltic Sea islands, but only six are inhabited. Two of them are easily accessible by train.

Rügen, the largest German island, is famous for its sandy beaches and dramatic chalk cliffs. On some days, direct ICE trains run from Berlin to Ostseebad Binz, the island's main seaside resort with its long beach and elegant villas. From Sassnitz station, you can take one of Germany's most scenic hikes through Jasmund National Park, along the cliffs to the Königsstuhl viewpoint. The island's local trains also reach Prora, where the Nazis built a massive seaside resort in the 1930s, designed to host up to 20,000 holidaymakers.

Usedom, the second largest island, was once known as "Berlin's beach." Its imperial spas—Ahlbeck, Heringsdorf, and Bansin—were historically connected to the German capital by direct train. Today, you transfer at Züssow, where the diesel-powered Usedomer Bäderbahn runs toward Świnoujście in Poland. After crossing the Peenestrom on a bright blue drawbridge, the scenic 1.5-hour route takes you across the island.

In the coastal towns, the imperial era comes alive through monumental white villas along the shore and in the town centres, once holiday retreats for Berlin's elite. In Peenemünde, reachable via a branch line from Zinnowitz, you can see where the Nazis launched their first rocket into space in 1942.

SUPER SLOW

16 The Douro Valley
Porto - Pocinho (3.5 hours)

The Douro Valley journey begins in Porto, whose historic centre is a UNESCO World Heritage Site, and departs from Porto São Bento, one of Europe's most beautiful stations, famed for its blue-and-white azulejo tiles. From the city, the railway follows the Douro east, linking the terraced wine landscapes of the Alto Douro with the remote interior. Originally built to transport wine from the vineyards to the coast, the line now unfolds at a gentler pace. For three and a half hours to Pocinho, the river remains a constant companion, vineyards rise in steep terraces, and the scenery grows steadily wilder. It's a slow, immersive journey through one of Portugal's most celebrated landscapes.

17 Settle-Carlisle Line
Leeds - Carlisle (2.5 hours)

This route carries you through seventeen stations across the beautiful Yorkshire Dales and Cumbrian Mountains. Its highlight is the final stretch between Settle and Carlisle, one of the most scenic railway journeys in Britain. From Settle, the train climbs quickly onto the high fells, opening up broad views across the hills and the villages below. The standout moment is the crossing of Ribblehead Viaduct, a 24-arch stone bridge that soars above the valley floor. Beyond it, the line runs through the wild, remote moorland of the Pennines, passing lonely stations and vast, empty stretches of open country.

The Douro Valley

18 Ligne des Horlogers
*Besançon-Viotte - Morteau
(1 hour, 20 mins)*

This gentle rural run crosses the French Jura through winding river valleys and wooded hills. The 75 km (46.5 mi) route follows the River Doubs for much of the way, stopping in old villages such as Valdahon and Gilley before reaching Morteau, a small town known for its traditional watchmaking.

19 Rauma Line
Dombås - Åndalsnes (1.5 hours)

Train journeys in Norway are beautiful everywhere – the Bergen-Oslo route is world-famous – but this shorter 115 km (71.5 mi) route deserves a place on any list of Europe's great railways. It follows the long, narrow Romsdal valley to the Romsdalsfjord, passing waterfalls, sheer cliffs and the emerald-green Rauma River as it cuts through wild and dramatic terrain.

The line crosses 32 bridges, including the famous Kylling Bridge. At the Vermafossen waterfall, the train slows down so that passengers can take a photo of the water crashing down the mountainside, almost close enough to touch.

The final stretch is the most striking. Here the train runs beneath the Trollveggen, Europe's tallest vertical rock face, rising 1,100 m (3,610 ft) above the valley floor.

20 Centovalli Railway
Locarno - Domodossola (2 hours)

The century-old Vigezzina–Centovalli Railway links Italy's Vigezzo Valley with Switzerland's Centovalli, the "Hundred Valleys". Starting in Locarno on Lake Maggiore, the train crosses 83 bridges and passes through 31 tunnels, travelling past steep vineyards, chestnut forests and untouched valleys.

Among the highlights are the steel bridge over the River Isorno at Intragna and the Ruinacci Bridge at Camedo. Intragna itself is a delight to explore, with its stone houses, elegant palazzi and the tallest bell tower in Canton Ticino. Between Intragna and Camedo, near the Italian border, a walking path follows the old Via del Mercato. Or stay on board to Domodossola, a welcoming Italian town that marks the end of the line.

21 Train des Merveilles
Nice - Tende (2 hours, 15 mins)

This unforgettable ride cuts through the rugged Alpes-Maritimes, following a medieval salt route that climbs 1,000 m (3,280 ft) in just 70 km (43.5 mi). The line crosses around a hundred bridges and viaducts and almost as many tunnels and spiral loops. Its name, the Train of Wonders, refers to the thousands of ancient rock carvings found in the mountains above Tende.

Leipzig Hauptbahnhof

Pinzgauer Lokalbahn

22 Le Train Jaune
Villefranche-de-Conflent - Latour-de-Carol (3 hours)

The famous canary-yellow train, also known as the Ligne de Cerdagne, runs 62 km (38.5 mi) through the Pyrenees, climbing to Bolquère-Eyne, which at 1,593 m (5,226 ft) is the highest SNCF station in France. Some of the carriages are more than a century old, and in summer you can ride in open-air coaches.

It's also one of Europe's most sustainable railways. Two hydroelectric dams were built in 1910 specifically to power the line, and they still provide its electricity today. When you arrive at Latour-de-Carol, take a moment to look around. Nowhere else in the world do three track gauges meet in one place: French standard gauge, Spanish broad gauge and the narrow-gauge Train Jaune.

23 Pinzgauer Lokalbahn
Zell am See - Krimml (1.5 hours)

Zell am See is one of those picture-perfect Austrian towns, set on the edge of its lake with mountains rising behind it. From here, a small narrow-gauge train sets off into the Alps on what is easily one of the most charming railway journeys in the country. The Pinzgauer Lokalbahn follows the River Salzach through the Pinzgau valley for around ninety minutes, finishing in Krimml, home to the largest waterfalls in Central Europe.

The line has 38 stations, most of them request stops. Many are little more than a wooden shelter, but they're in such beautiful locations that it's hard not to get off and explore each one. If you do, remember to press the button on the platform as the next train approaches, otherwise it'll sail straight past.

The train is especially popular with walkers heading for the Hohe Tauern National Park and the Kitzbühel Alps. In summer, bicycles are allowed on board, making it a convenient way to reach the start of the Tauern Cycle Path in Krimml. Flooding in 2021 damaged the section between Niedernsill and Krimml, which remains closed. Replacement buses run instead.

Rauma river near Åndalsnes, Norway

Night Trains

Europe's Best Overnight Services

After decades in decline, Europe's night trains are making a comeback. As more travellers look for sustainable alternatives to flying, overnight rail travel has found a new audience. The appeal is clear: private compartments for two, three or four people, your own bed, sometimes your own facilities, and the simple pleasure of falling asleep in one city and waking up in another. Night trains had their golden age in the 1960s and '70s, when legendary services like the Night Riviera and Le Train Bleu linked Europe's great cities. You could travel from Paris to Rome, London to Nice, and cross the continent in a sleeping carriage. Then came the high-speed era, and overnight trains almost vanished. Now, thankfully, they are returning. The Austrian Railways (ÖBB) have played a key role in the renaissance of night trains, reintroducing many international connections and running state-of-the-art new trains on some routes, making Vienna once again a major hub for overnight travel.

When night trains make sense

A night train can feel like a hotel room on wheels, with your own cabin, your own bed, and sometimes even a private bathroom and shower, making it a comfortable way to cover long distances while also saving on hotel costs. Some routes even offer a form of room service.

Across Europe there are now roughly 100 night train routes, although the exact number changes as some services run only at certain times of year. But not every overnight journey is worth taking. Some routes are simply too short to allow for proper rest, and nobody wants to be woken at five in the morning and sent out into the cold before the day has properly begun. The best connections combine sensible departure times with enough hours for real sleep and arrivals that are late enough for you to step off the train and head straight to a cafe.

To make an overnight journey memorable rather than merely practical, you need time not only to sleep, but also to settle into your cabin, unwind from the day, and enjoy the quiet, gently moving world of the train at night.

OUR FAVOURITE ROUTES

Amsterdam or Brussels to Vienna

A superb way to reach the Austrian capital. Trains depart around 7:30pm from both cities, arriving in Vienna just before 9:30am. The timetable gives you enough time to sleep properly, and you arrive ready for a Viennese breakfast.

Amsterdam to Prague

The European Sleeper runs overnight from Brussels via Amsterdam to Berlin, and since 2024 continues to Dresden and Prague. This Dutch startup is bringing night trains back to routes that lost them years ago. But the Brussels-to-Prague connection is new: no direct train has made this journey before, crossing four countries and four capitals in one go.

The best part might be waking up. As the train approaches Dresden, the Elbe River opens up below, the historic old town spreading along its banks with the Frauenkirche rising above the rooftops. Past Dresden, the route gets better. From Heidenau, the tracks follow the Elbe through Saxon Switzerland, with dramatic rock formations and the river winding below. It's only 30 minutes, but it's one of the most beautiful stretches of railway in Germany, especially in early morning when mist hangs over the water. Just past Stadt Wehlen, you can also spot the Bastei Bridge on the far bank.

Hamburg to Stockholm

Travel to Hamburg by day, have dinner by the River Alster or in the St Georg district, then board the SJ EuroNight north. Departures are usually after 9pm, with arrival in Stockholm around 10am. Southbound, the train leaves Stockholm in the early evening and reaches Hamburg between 6 and 7am.

Stockholm to Narvik

One of the great rail journeys of Europe. The 18.5-hour trip from Stockholm into the Arctic Circle and onward to Narvik is slow travel at its finest. With no Wi-Fi, the focus is on forests, mountains, lakes and the beauty of Lapland. In summer, long daylight hours mean you won't miss the scenery. The two-person cabins are comfortable, the showers clean, and the café-bar is ideal for meeting fellow travellers over a Swedish beer while spotting reindeer from the window. This is everything a night train should be. (See page 13.)

London to Scotland: The Caledonian Sleeper

Every night except Saturday, the Caledonian Sleeper leaves London Euston around 9pm for destinations across Scotland. The Fort William service, for instance, arrives around 11am, giving you a full night's rest.

Falling asleep after a gin and tonic in the club car and waking in the Highlands is a joy. The train offers good meals and breakfasts served with views of lochs and mountains. It remains one of Europe's great rail experiences. (See page 59.)

Paris to Nice & Hendaye

French night trains are returning. SNCF now runs overnight services from Paris to Nice, Toulouse and Hendaye, with more planned. It's a welcome reversal after two decades of decline. The Hendaye service is especially appealing. You leave Paris in the evening and wake up on the edge of the Basque Country, where the Atlantic meets the foothills of the Pyrenees.

Other notable routes

- Vienna - Budapest - Bucharest
- Munich to Ljubljana and Zagreb – a comfortable sleeper through the Alps into the Balkans
- Helsinki - Rovaniemi - Santa Claus Expressi to the capital of Lapland
- Milan to Sicily – includes the unique ferry crossing of the Strait of Messina
- Munich to Rome – a classic route through the Alps and down towards the capital

Interrail & Eurail Passes

One ticket, unlimited European travel

Believe it or not, it's still entirely possible to travel from London to Athens, or from Algeciras on Spain's southern tip to Narvik, far above the Arctic Circle in Norway – some 5,000 km (3,100 mi) – on a single ticket. Since 1972, Interrail & Eurail have been a rite of passage for generations of travellers. With over 33,000 stations to choose from, you're free to craft your own journey through Europe, one stop at a time.

THE SPIRIT OF INTERRAIL & EURAIL

Few travel experiences offer the same blend of freedom and connection as Interrail & Eurail. It's not just about getting from A to B–it's about the journey itself. Whether you're setting off on your first European adventure or returning to the rails, Interrail & Eurail remain one of the simplest, most flexible and most rewarding ways to explore the continent. Buy a pass, hop on a train, and see where the tracks take you. Go beyond the well-known destinations and uncover thousands of lesser-known corners of Europe.

CHOOSING THE RIGHT PASS

Interrail and Eurail are essentially the same pass. The only difference is who they're for: Eurail is for travellers who live outside Europe, while Interrail is for European residents. Just note that if you're from Europe, you can't use the pass for travel within your own country.
As for the passes themselves, you can choose between a One Country Pass – ideal if you want to focus on a single destination – and the Global Pass, which gives you free rein across 33 European countries. More information is available at interrail.eu or eurail.com. The Global Pass comes in two versions, continuous and flexible.

Continuous passes let you travel as much as you like for 15 days, 22 days, or one, two, or three months. If you're planning a long trip with lots of train journeys, this is the simplest choice.

Flexible passes, however, are more popular as they suit a wider range of travel styles. You choose a set number of travel days within a longer period, either 4, 5 or 7 travel days within one month, or 10 or 15 travel days within two months. This allows rest days, longer stays, and spontaneous side trips (using separate, inexpensive tickets) without using up your entire pass.

OUTBOUND & INBOUND JOURNEYS

You can't use your pass for unlimited travel within your country of residence. So, if you live in the UK, for instance, you won't be able to hop on and off trains freely there. However, your pass does include one outbound and inbound journey, allowing you to travel once from your home station to the border and once back again.

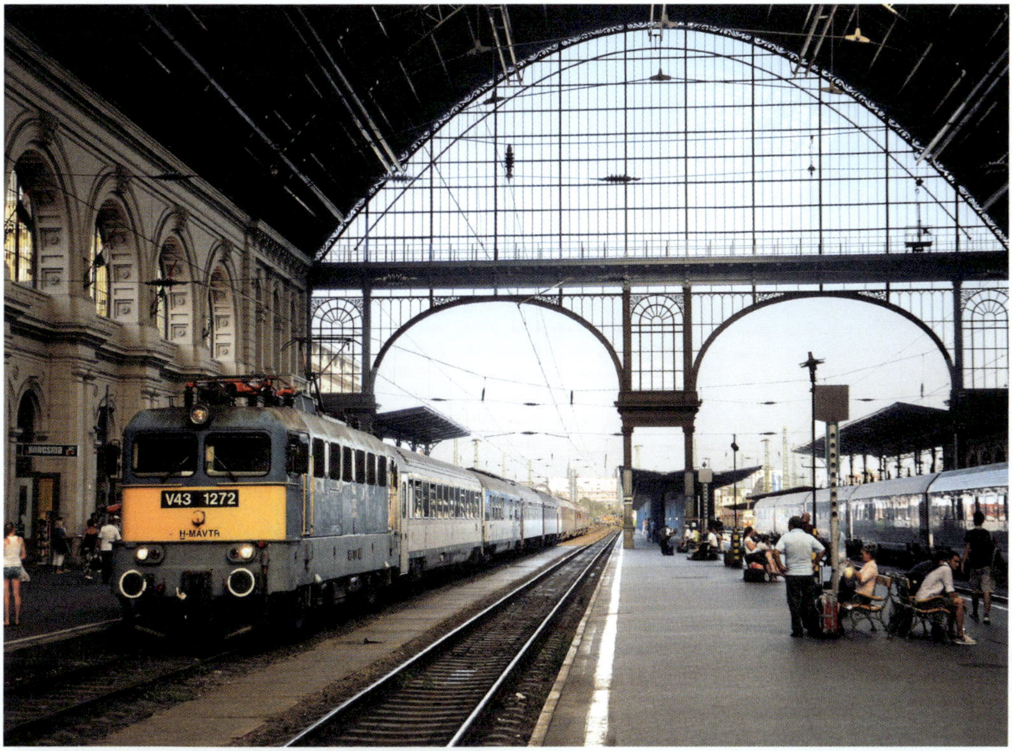
V43 1272
H-MÁVTR

Laissez-vous rêver

NORD
NORD

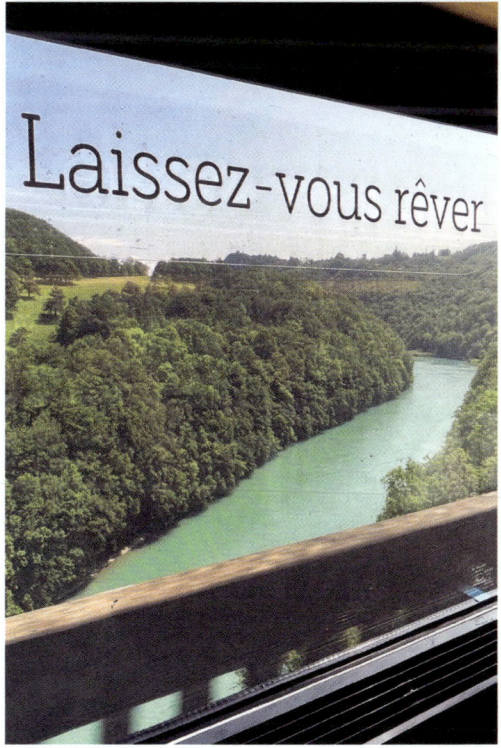

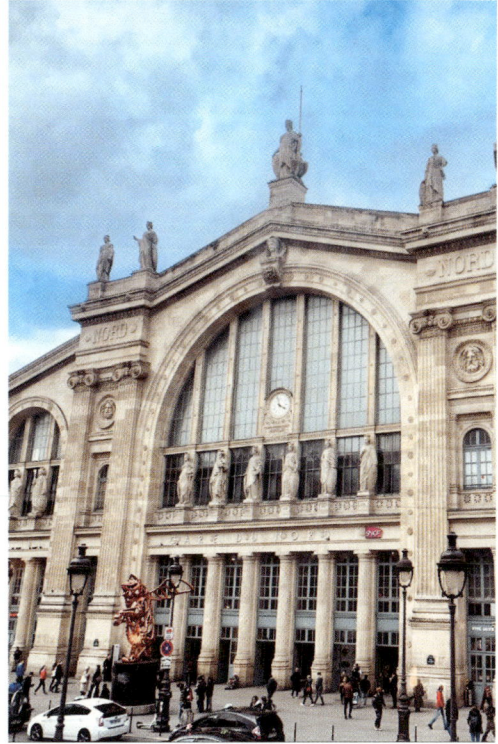

NOT JUST FOR THE YOUNG

Anyone can purchase a pass, regardless of age. Children 11 and younger travel free, and there are generous discounts for travellers 27 and younger and over 60.

WHEN TO TRAVEL

The best time to go is outside the peak summer months (July and August) and school holiday periods. Trains are quieter then, and accommodation tends to be more affordable too.

COMPARE PRICES

For some longer round trips, for example to Southern Europe, a four- or five-day Interrail/Eurail Pass can quickly work out cheaper than a standard return ticket.

WHEN A PASS MAKES SENSE, AND WHEN IT DOESN'T

If you plan ahead, you can sometimes snap up cheap individual tickets: London to Paris or Amsterdam to Berlin for under €40, for example. But if you value flexibility and spontaneity, an Interrail Pass is hard to beat, particularly for longer, multi-country itineraries.

If you plan to travel extensively within one or more Western European country, you'll likely save money with an Interrail Pass, as last-minute fares in places like the UK, Norway, Germany, Switzerland, and Austria tend to be steep. France often has advance-purchase deals on long-distance routes, though not for regional trains, so Interrail can still be the more economical option. If your trip is mostly in Eastern Europe, local train tickets tend to be cheaper, so buying them individually may cost less overall. But it's still wise to book well in advance.

RESERVATIONS: WHEN DO YOU NEED THEM?

Although the Global Pass gives you plenty of freedom, some trains require seat reservations on top of the pass. This is most common on high-speed and long-distance services in France, Spain and Italy. In many other countries, such as Germany, Switzerland, Austria and the Netherlands, you can usually just board without a reservation, though night trains and tourist routes like the Bernina Express and Glacier Express are exceptions.

You can book reservations through interrail.eu once you've purchased your pass, with prices typically ranging from €5 to €40 depending on the route and train type. It's worth reserving early for popular journeys like Paris–Barcelona or London–Amsterdam, especially in summer or on weekends, as the demand is very high. On Eurostar trains, seat numbers for pass holders are limited.

If you've got the time and don't mind taking slower routes, you can travel almost anywhere without reservations by using regional trains, or high-speed services in countries where reservations aren't required. The Rail Planner app clearly shows which trains need reservations and which don't, making it easy to plan around them.

PLANNING YOUR JOURNEY

The Rail Planner app is your go-to tool. It lists train connections across Europe, works offline, shows which routes require reservations, and lets you save journeys for quick reference. The Deutsche Bahn website (bahn.de) is also excellent for checking timetables and connections.

BUYING SINGLE TICKETS

Unfortunately, there is still no single website that allows you to book every international train journey across Europe, but several platforms come close, including trainline.com, raileurope.com, omio.com and happyrail.com. These websites sell both domestic and cross border tickets for many European countries, and some also offer Interrail and Eurail passes, including seat reservations.

For domestic trips or simple cross border journeys between neighbouring countries, for example between Germany and France, the best fares often come directly from the national railway operators, like in this case Deutsche Bahn.

HELPFUL TIPS BEFORE YOU GO

Plan loosely, not rigidly. Have a rough route in mind, but don't lock yourself into a tight schedule. Half the joy of Interrail is changing your plans on a whim.

Book reservations early for popular routes. France's TGV, Spain's AVE and many Scandinavian night trains sell out quickly. Reserve as soon as you know your dates, especially in summer. It's also better to book too many reservations than too few.

Take it slow. Save money by avoiding trains that require reservations. Opt for slower and often more scenic routes without high-speed trains and make the journey part of the experience. Add unexpected stops along the way and use the Rail Planner app to search for connections marked 'no seat reservations required' or maximise transfer times for spontaneous discoveries..

Embrace the unexpected. Wherever you are in Europe, head to the nearest station and board the first train leaving from platform 2. See where you end up…

Be an early bird. Early trains are quieter, cleaner, and, in our experience, less prone to delays. Plus, the morning light is beautiful.

Pack light. A backpack or small wheeled bag makes connections and platform changes much easier.

Use night trains. They save you a night's accommodation and maximise your sightseeing time. Plus, with a flexible pass, an overnight journey counts as just one travel day, even though it spans two.

Choose base cities for day trips. Instead of moving every day, pick a hub and explore from there. From Berlin you can reach Leipzig, Dresden or the Baltic coast. From Florence, Siena, Pisa and the Tuscan hill towns are all within easy reach. You'll see more and feel far less worn out.

Arrive early at major stations. Platform changes are common, especially at big stations. Give yourself time to navigate, grab a coffee, or simply enjoy the architecture.

Bring provisions. Not every train has a dining car, and not every dining car is worth the price. Pack snacks and water, especially for long journeys.

ROUTES WITHOUT RESERVATIONS

For the ultimate sense of freedom, choose routes that don't require seat reservations. From Amsterdam or Brussels, for example, you can travel freely through Germany, Switzerland, Austria, Hungary, and the Czech Republic. Along the way, you'll pass through beautiful cities and landscapes, including the Alps and the Elbe Valley. With a Global Pass valid for ten travel days within two months, you could follow an itinerary like this:

Brussels – Frankfurt (4 hrs)
Frankfurt – Freiburg – Basel – Zurich (4 hrs)
Zurich – Innsbruck – Graz (9.5 hrs)
Graz – Budapest (5 hrs)
Budapest – Vienna (2.5 hrs)
Vienna – Brno – Prague (4 hrs)
Prague – Dresden – Berlin (4 hrs)
Berlin – Amsterdam (6 hrs), reservations required in summer only.

WHO MADE THIS BOOK?

BART GIEPMANS

Bart is an author, travel journalist, and photographer with a lifelong love of trains. At twelve, his father gave him an NS (Dutch Railways) annual pass so he could discover the Netherlands by rail, the beginning of a European journey that has never truly ended. An Erasmus exchange in Chambéry, followed by years living in Utrecht, Amsterdam, Paris, and Munich, and since 2011 in Berlin, have made him European through and through.

His professional journey in the railways began as a steward on the night train to the Alps, followed by communications roles at NS, Deutsche Bahn, and as a freelance consultant for Eurail. In 2023, he was named Travel Journalist of the Year in the Netherlands. Today, Bart continues to crisscross Europe by train, drawn to the slower pace, the grandeur of historic stations, and a firm belief that sustainable travel is not only more beautiful, but also the future.

WILLIAM SIMPSON

William is a keen traveller with a particular love for rail adventures, a passion sparked in childhood by night trains to Cornwall and day trips to Paris on the Eurostar. As a teenager, an Interrail pass opened up Europe and set him on a path he's followed ever since. The rails have carried him across continents: through Ukraine, across China from east to west, along the Trans-Siberian Railway from Beijing to Moscow, and through Central Asia, where trains remain one of the most revealing ways to experience a place.
For this book, he travelled through Scotland and Wales, seeking out routes where the journey is as exciting as the destination. He has lived in Berlin since 2019, with earlier stints in Beijing, Shanghai, and Madrid.

INDEX

TRAINS & ROUTES

Ardennes, Through the 244
Bergensbanen 238
Bernina Express 240
Black Forest railway 34
Brenner Route 198, 245
Caledonian Sleeper 60, 260
Cambrian Main Line 120
Centovalli Railway 252
Circumvesuviana 135
EuroCity Geneva-Milan 244
European Sleeper 259
Far North Line 62
Ferrocarril de Sóller 246
Ferrovia Circumetnea 136
Frecciarossa 133
Glacier Express 241
Golden-Pass Express 182, 244
Gotthard line 130
Harzer Schmalspurbahnen 158
Hungaria 238
Hungerburgbahn 198
Inlandsbanan 13-27
Intercity Notte (to Sicily) 133
Iron Ore Line 15
Jungfrau Railway 179 - 185
Ligne des Horlogers 252
Matterhorn Gotthard Railway 38
Mont-Blanc Express 245
Montenegro Express 239
Nordlandsbanan 27
Ofoten Rail 26
Pinzgauer Lokalbahn 255
Rauma Line 252
Rhaetian Railway 38, 240
Scotrail 62-71

Semmering Railway 240
Settle-Carlisle Line 251
SJ EuroNight 260
Snowdonian Mountain Railway 126
Tatra Electric Railway 148-153
TGV Méditerranée 75
Torre del Oro 240
Train de la côte bleue 85
Train des Merveilles 87, 252
Train des Pignes 87
Train Jaune, Le 255
Transalpin 239
Trenino Verde 246
Usedomer Bäderbahn 250
Valsugana Line 202
Wadden Sea, Crossing The 246
West Highland Line 68, 70

LIST OF COUNTRIES

Austria 142-155, 166-177, 197-205, 239, 240, 245, 255
Belgium 244, 259
Croatia 166-177
Czechia 44-57
France 44-57, 72-87, 88-101, 104-117, 208-217, 218-237, 245, 246, 252, 255, 260
Germany 28-41, 44-57, 156-165, 166-177, 187-195, 197-205, 238, 245, 246, 250, 260
Italy 104-117, 128-141, 197-205, 244, 245, 246, 252
Luxembourg 244
Morocco 218-237
Montenegro 239
The Netherlands, 259, 265
Norway 12-27, 238, 252, 260
Poland 44-57

Portugal 251
Scotland 58-71, 260
Serbia 239
Slovakia 142-155
Slovenia 171, 177
Spain 88-101, 208-217, 218-237, 240
Sweden 12-27, 260
Switzerland 28-41, 128-141, 178-185, 239, 240, 241, 244, 245
United Kingdom 44-57, 58-71, 118-127, 260
Wales 118-127

LIST OF PLACES & STATIONS

Aberaeron 121
Aberystwyth 121
Abisko 26
Albenga 116
Andernach 31
Arctic circle 22
Arles 85

Bacharach 33
Baltic Islands 250
Basel 34
Beaulieu 112
Beaune 76, 80
Bedous 209, 214
Bergun 240
Berlin 55, 187
Bern 180
Bingen 33
Bodø 27
Bonn 31
Bordeaux 210, 212
Bratislava 146
Buddnakk 22

Caen 48
Canfranc 209, 214, 217
Catania 129, 136
Chur 38
Cinque Terre 116
Cologne 29, 30
Corniglia 116
Corrour 70
Corsica 246
Criccieth 126

Douro Valley 251
Dresden, 238, 260
Dunnet Bay 64

Etna, Mount 136, 141

Fès 228, 233
Figueres 96
Filisur 240
Fort William 66, 70
Frankfurt 167, 168

Gällivare 24
Gdańsk 188, 190, 192
Genoa 116
Glasgow 66
Glenfinnan 70
Goslar 158
Graz 239
Grindelwald 182

Hannover 157
Heidelberg 34
Hendaye 260

Innsbruck 198
Interlaken 182
Intragna 252
Inverness 62, 66

John O'Groats 65
Jokkmokk 20, 22, 24

Karlsruhe 34
Kénitra 228
Kiruna 25
Koblenz 31
Košice 143
Kraków 54, 192
Krimml 255

Latour-de-Carol 255
Lauterbrunnen 182, 185
Levico 202, 205
Liège 244
London 46, 60
Lugano 133
Luxembourg 244
Lyon 80

Mainz 33
Malbork 192
Mallaig 70
Mallorca 246
Manarola 116
Marrakech 233, 235
Marseille 85
Menton 112
Milan 130, 244
Monaco 112
Monterosso 116
Montpellier 89
Mora 15, 18
Munich 198

Naples 133
Narvik 15, 26, 27, 260
Nice 85, 106
Nuremberg 51

Oberalp Pass 38
Oberwesel 33
Orkney 65
Östersund 20
Oświęcim 54

Paris 51, 73, 75, 210, 219
Pau 210
Peenemünde 250
Pisa 117
Pochino 251
Poprad 148, 153
Portbou 90, 96
Portmeirion 126
Portsmouth 47
Poznań 188, 192
Prague 52
Prora 250
Pwllheli 126

Randazzo 141
Remagen 31
Riksgränsen 26
Riomaggiore 116

Romsdalsfjord 252
Ronda 220
Rügen 250

San Remo 115
Sardinia 246
Sassnitz 250
Schaffhausen 38
Semmering 240
Šibenik 176
Sicily 246
Sitges 98
Snowdonia 125, 126
Split 167, 173, 176
Stockholm 15, 260
Storuman 20
Sylt 246

Tangier 227
Taormina 135
Tarifa 219, 224
Tarragona 98
Tende 87, 252
Thun 180
Thurso 64
Tremadog 125
Trenčín 146, 148
Trento 201, 202, 205

Usedom 250

Valencia 100
Ventimiglia 115
Vernazza 116
Vesuvius, Mount 135
Vienna 144, 259
Vilhelmina Norra 20
Villefranche-sur-Mer 110

Warsaw 192
Wernigerode 158, 160

Zagreb 168, 171
Zakopane 192
Zaragoza 217
Zell am See 239, 255
Zurich 38, 129

SLOW TRAVEL EUROPE — PLATFORM EUROPE

Slow Travel Europe is a concept by
mo'media publishers

Text
Bart Giepmans and William Simpson

Photography
Bart Giepmans

Cover
Le Côte Bleue, France, photo Raik Bäumler

Art direction
Jelle F. Post

Other photography
Gerdien Barnard (p.177), Tim Bilman (p.210), Mikal de Bont (p.96), Jeroen Elkhuizen (p.84, 92, 113), Doro Engels (p.250), Guus Ferree (p.156, 160, 162), Michael Gentschy (p.268), Andreas Hundt (p.154, 155), Robbie Kammeijer (p.67, 71), Mark Kohn (p.159), Bernd Lemmermann (p.30), Anja Martin (p.204), Shirley Nieuwland (p.215), Florian Schomburg (p.36, 39, 241), Bjorn Snelders (p.68, 242), William Simpson (Scotland, Wales), Henrik Tjidefärd (p.15, 19, 22, 25, 26), back-on-track.eu (p.258), Bern Tourismus (p.181), Eurail (p.82-83, 168, 263).

Special thanks to
Raik Bäumler (for being such a wonderfully grumpy model), Gerdien Barnard, Nicky Gardner, Susanne Kries, Martin Speer, the Eurail team in Utrecht, and all our travel companions along the way.

Editing
William Simpson

All rights reserved
No part of this book may be copied, displayed, extracted, reproduced, utilised, stored in a retrieval system or transmitted in any form or by any means, electronic, mechanical or otherwise including but not limited to photocopying, recording, or scanning without the prior written permission of the publisher. No part of this book may be used or reproduced in any manner for the purpose of training artificial intelligence technologies or systems.

Publishers' Note
Every effort has been made to ensure that the information in this book is accurate at the time of going to press. The publisher welcomes any information or suggestions for correction or improvement. Please send us an email at info@momedia.nl.

Authors' Note
The routes in this book are just the beginning. We're always discovering new journeys and sharing travel tips on our website at railtripping.com. Follow us on Instagram @railtripping for regular inspiration, beautiful photography, and stories from the rails. We'd love to hear about your own adventures too.

Disclaimer
Train travel means that itineraries, routes, and timetables change frequently. You are responsible for your own journey. Proper preparation and up-to-date information are essential. The author and publisher cannot be held liable for accidents, injuries, or losses that may occur while following the routes described in this book.

© 2022, 2024, Dutch edition, Uitgeverij FJORD
This book contains revised and updated stories from two of our books.
Original titles: *Perron Europa – Op reis met de trein* and *Perron Europa 2 – Nog meer op reis met de trein*

Text: Bart Giepmans and others
Photography: Bart Giepmans and others
Editing and corrections: Gerdien Barnard and others
Art direction: Jelle F. Post

© 2026, English translation, mo'media publishers
Translation: William Simpson
Art direction: Jelle F. Post

Slow Travel Europe – Platform Europe
ISBN 978 94 9333 884 5
NUR 500, 508, 510

Slow Travel Europe
Also available in this series: *Hiking Trails* (the most beautiful long-distance hikes in 18 European countries) and *Going North* (inspiring travel stories from Denmark, Sweden and Norway).

MOMEDIAPUBLISHERS.COM